First-Time Mom: Prepare Yourself for Pregnancy

New Mom's Survival Handbook with All the Helpful Tips and Information That You Need While Expecting + 30 Day Meal Plan for Pregnancy

Table of Contents

Introduction 6

Chapter 1 - The Journey Begins 9

    An Essential Quit List for All Pregnant Women 9

    The Truth About Weight Gain During Pregnancy 13

    What About Stretch Marks? 15

    5 Health-Boosting Supplements for Mom and Baby 18

Chapter 2 - The First Trimester 22

    10 Common Symptoms of the First Trimester & How to Manage Them 23

    When to Call Your Doctor 27

    5 Ways Your Body Will Change in the First Trimester 29

    What is a Doula & How Can They Help? 30

Chapter 3 - The Second Trimester 34

    Pelvic Floor Exercises that All Mothers Must Know 35

    5 Ways to Start Bonding With Your Baby 37

    Watch Out For These Signs of Preeclampsia 38

    The Best Ways to Exercise in the Second Trimester 40

    10 Fun Ideas for the Second Trimester 41

Chapter 4 - The Third Trimester 46

    Every First-Time Mom's To-Do List for the Third Trimester ... 46

    Breastfeeding vs. Formula Feeding 49

    Tackling Third-Trimester Insomnia 51

Labor Signals & What They Mean 53

Braxton Hicks Contractions vs. Labor Contractions 55

How Do You Induce Labor Safely and Naturally? 56

Chapter 5 - Preparing for the Big Day 58

Pack These 13 Essentials in Your Hospital Bag 58

22 New-Baby & First-Time Mom Necessities 61

How to Start Creating a Birth Plan 69

Chapter 6 - Childbirth & Labor 72

10 Less-Known Things You Should Know About Vaginal Childbirth & Labor 72

4 Things to Do for a Safer C-Section 76

The Lowdown on Epidural Anesthesia 77

7 Helpful Tricks for Pushing that Baby Out 79

The Best Positions for Pushing with an Epidural 80

7 Little-Known Things about C-Sections 81

Chapter 7 - Postpartum Care 83

What Every Mother Needs to Do after Giving Birth 83

9 Completely Normal Long-Term & Short-Term Effects of Pregnancy and Childbirth 85

How to Help the Body Heal from Birth 88

Everything You Need to Know About Postpartum Depression 90

9 Soul-Soothing Self-Care Ideas for a First-Time Mom 91

Chapter 8 - Your Newborn Baby 95

11 Things You Should Know About Newborn Babies 95

    6 Must-Know Rules About Formula-Feeding 97

    Foods to Limit or Avoid While Breastfeeding 99

    How to Prevent Sudden Infant Death Syndrome 101

    It's Bath Time! 103

Conclusion **107**

30 Day Meal Plan **110**

    Week 1 110

    Week 2 111

    Week 3 113

    Week 4 114

    Week 5 116

    Snack List 117

Introduction

You're about to become a mother for the first time – congratulations! These months will be some of the most special in your entire life and also, some of the most challenging. As overjoyed as you are to be bringing a new life into the world, chances are you're also incredibly nervous. Carrying a child is no walk in the park, as you've likely heard. And when it's your first time, it's all new and uncertain territory. You're probably anxious about the ways your body is changing, the new sensations you're experiencing, and above all, you're wondering how on earth you can keep your baby healthy when there is such an overload of information about what to do and not do. If you're feeling overwhelmed by this new chapter in your life, no one would blame you.

Thing is, pregnancy does not have to be a time of confusion and anxiety. This may be an entirely new experience, but that doesn't mean it has to be fraught with worry. All you need is the right guidance and helpful, accurate information that is easily accessible to you at all times. With this book by your side, you can transition confidently into your role as a first-time mom. Each chapter will guide you through the many steps of your pregnancy, so you'll never feel uncertain. No more stress or anxiety. Just total awareness and all the preparation you need to be the most competent mom for your new baby.

In this book, each trimester will be completely demystified. I'll get in-depth about each specific trimester and what your baby needs from you in each one. You'll understand your symptoms, how to manage them, activities to avoid at all costs, what to eat for your baby's optimal health, how to prepare for labor and birth – and so much more. If you have a question, I have an answer. Just take a peek in this book whenever you're not sure about something.

As the proud mom of five beautiful and healthy children, it's safe to say I am very experienced when it comes to pregnancy and baby care. I vividly remember what it was like to be pregnant for the first time – I devoured a heap of books, frustrated that I couldn't find *just one book* to cover everything. For over a decade I coached friends through their first pregnancies, began the popular 'Happy Mom, Happy Baby' club in my hometown, and of course, I expanded my knowledge as each of my other babies came along. No two pregnancies are alike – but what I've learned is that the best advice and support always comes from an experienced mom.

With the best advice under your belt, you'll ride the waves of pregnancy with confidence. You can focus on your own physical and emotional well-being so that, when your baby comes, he or she is brought into the best possible environment. No mom will tell you that pregnancy is easy, but what it *can* be is a clarifying and empowering experience for the lifetime of motherhood that is to come. With this book, you'll have all the tools you need to get on the right path.

The people I coach and the friends I've supported through first-time pregnancies continue to thank me to this day. While every mom knows there's no such thing as a pregnancy 'expert,' I've been told I come as close as you can get. The secrets I share with the people I help are exactly what I will be unveiling in this book. You, too, can reap the benefits I've seen other mothers blossom with.

When it comes to your pregnancy preparation, there's no such thing as doing it later. Your budding baby needs specific conditions *now*; you're either preparing or you're not. The early days are some of the most crucial for your baby's development, as you are still at risk of a miscarriage. Make sure you get the right help as soon as possible, so you can get your baby on the path towards optimal health.

The chance to be a good mom doesn't just arise when your baby is born; the chance is here already. It is now. The choices you make while your child is in your belly have the potential to affect his or her entire life. Don't stumble into motherhood. Take strong, empowered steps. As you turn the page, feel assured that the first strong step begins.

Chapter 1 - The Journey Begins

With a decade of pregnancy coaching behind me, I've noticed many similarities between all first-time moms, especially in the early days. Once the thrill and joy from their good news has settled, they have the same concerns. "How much do I have to change my current lifestyle?" is the general gist of most of their questions. They ask me, "How can I stop myself from gaining so much weight?" or "How can I prevent stretch marks?" New moms tend to feel guilty for asking these questions, but there's no reason to! A baby changes everything and that includes your body. It's okay to have moments where you feel overwhelmed – where it feels like the world is shifting under your feet. Be patient with yourself and know that it's a lot easier to navigate when you take it one step at a time.

In this chapter, I'll cover all the first concerns that I've heard from first-time moms. Everything you need to know right off the bat is here, as it'll likely apply to your entire pregnancy. The journey has begun – embrace it!

An Essential Quit List for All Pregnant Women

When you're pregnant, the last thing you should be doing is business as usual. You are no longer the only person affected by your diet and habits; there's a new life on board now. And in some cases, 'business as usual' can have disastrous consequences on the new life you're creating. Once you know you're expecting, you'll need to cull every single habit that's on this quit list. This is non-negotiable. It's absolutely essential that you and your baby are safe and healthy.

1. **Smoking and Second-Hand Smoke**

Smoking can have an extremely negative impact on your baby's health and your pregnancy as a whole. Pregnant women who smoke are much more likely to have a miscarriage, go through premature labor, or an ectopic pregnancy. And believe it or not, second-hand smoke is just as harmful. Exposure can lead to the same consequences as smoking and may even result in behavioral or learning issues in the growing child.

2. Chores that Involve Strong Chemicals and Fumes

Pregnant women don't get a free pass on all household chores but you should definitely avoid duties that involve heavy chemicals such as oven cleaners, aerosol products, and pesticides. It's difficult to steer clear of all chemicals – so if you're unsure if what you're using is safe, read the warning label and instructions. If you're the sole cleaner of the house, consider turning to natural options like baking soda and vinegar which can often do an equally efficient job. In addition to this, always wear rubber gloves when handling cleaning products and make sure a few windows are open so your home gets excellent ventilation. These practices can make all the difference!

3. All Alcohol

By now, quitting alcohol is well-known as an essential part of a healthy pregnancy – and for good reasons! When a pregnant woman drinks alcohol, it reaches her baby. This is because alcohol can pass through the bloodstream into the placenta. This can damage the baby's brain and organs, resulting in birth defects, brain damage, stillbirth, a miscarriage, and more. All types of alcohol must be avoided during pregnancy, including wine, beer, and liquor.

4. Over 200mg of Caffeine

You don't need to give up coffee or green tea entirely when you're expecting – but you should avoid consuming large amounts. Too much caffeine puts women at a higher risk of miscarriage. On top of this, studies have shown that caffeine can enter the placenta; this means that when you ingest caffeine, so does your baby. Caffeine may just give *you* a light buzz, but think of the effect it can have on a newly formed being without a developed metabolism. If you're a coffee drinker, limit yourself to one cup a day and no more. Keep in mind that many sodas and energy drinks also contain caffeine. If you enjoy drinking these types of beverages, pay close attention to how much caffeine they contain.

5. High-Mercury Fish

Fish can be highly beneficial for a pregnant woman's diet, but high-mercury fish are a whole different deal. Women who are pregnant or nursing are advised to steer clear of fish with high amounts of mercury in their meat. This means no tuna, shark, mackerel, and swordfish.

6. Unpasteurized Dairy Products

Pregnant women *and* infants should steer clear of unpasteurized dairy. In other words, anything made from raw milk such as unpasteurized cheese and obviously, raw milk itself. The pasteurization process kills harmful bacteria – so when you consume raw milk, there's a possibility it could contain dangerous microorganisms with the potential to pose life-threatening consequences to you and your child. A study published by the Minnesota Department of Public Health revealed that one in six people who drink raw milk will get sick. It is advised that all pregnant women play it safe and avoid consuming all forms of raw milk from any animal.

7. Cleaning Cat Litter

If you own a cat, pass the cat litter-cleaning duties to your partner, family member, or other housemates. As adorable as your cat is, he or she could be a carrier of the *Toxoplasma Gondii* parasite which could be transferred to you through contact with your cat's waste. This parasite can cause an infection called Toxoplasmosis and if you're infected while pregnant, it can result in big problems for the baby or your pregnancy, such as stillbirth or miscarriage. If there's no one else to change the cat litter, then take extra precautions by wearing gloves, only feeding your cat dry food, washing your hands thoroughly afterward and keeping your cat indoors.

8. Heavy-Lifting

Pregnant women should avoid all forms of heavy-lifting, as the strain caused can do different types of damage, depending on the trimester. In the first trimester, straining to lift heavy-objects may trigger a miscarriage. In later trimesters, the risks only increase. Due to hormone changes during pregnancy, the ligaments in a woman's pelvic floor and joints loosen; this makes them more prone to damage and stress. A weakened pelvic floor can lead to big problems with incontinence (inability to control urination) or even potentially lead to the womb collapsing into the vagina (prolapse). Although some women are more at risk than overs, a general rule of thumb is to avoid heavy lifting altogether and get someone to help you.

9. Some Types of Exercise

Exercise is highly recommended for all pregnant women, but certain types should be avoided. The following exercises present a variety of risks and are not suitable for pregnant women:

- Anything that involves jumping, bouncing, or leaping.

- Exercises with jerky movements or sudden direction changes.

- Contact sports such as soccer, boxing, basketball, or ice hockey.

- Abdominal exercises that involve lying on the back.

- Exercises that require lying on the stomach.

- Activities with a fall risk such as rock-climbing, skiing, gymnastics, and horseback riding.

10. Certain Over-the-Counter Medications

Pregnant women are advised against taking medication they used before pregnancy unless they speak to a doctor about it first. Many seemingly harmless over-the-counter medications, such as aspirin or ibuprofen, are incredibly risky during pregnancy. In the first trimester, they can bring about miscarriage and later on, they can lead to birth defects in your baby. A good rule of thumb is to always talk to your doctor before you use any type of medicine.

The Truth About Weight Gain During Pregnancy

It is well-known that weight gain should be expected during pregnancy. While the amount of weight gained will vary from woman to woman, there are many who gain a tremendous amount of weight and unfortunately, this prospect can worry some new mothers. Of course, new mothers shouldn't worry about how much weight they're gaining; as long as they and their babies are healthy, that's all that matters. Still, it's completely understandable if some moms want to watch their weight and in some cases, it may be advised.

Most mothers will not be obese during their pregnancy, which is the only time weight gain can become a significant risk. Mothers who are obese are at an increased risk of preeclampsia, gestational diabetes, and premature birth. So if you were already overweight prior to becoming pregnant, pay close attention to the following facts.

- **You don't need extra calories in your first and second trimester**

We've all heard the phrase 'eating for two' used in conjunction with a pregnant woman, but unknown to most, this does not refer to the amount of food eaten. Pregnant women do not need to eat twice as much in the first and second trimester. It's not calories they need more of, but nutrients. Instead of eating larger amounts, they need to be focusing on more nutrient-rich foods. The misconception around 'eating for two' can lead to a lot of needless weight gain.

- **How much weight you need to gain depends on your starting weight**

The average woman needs to gain between 25 and 35 lbs for a healthy pregnancy but some may need to gain less or more, depending on how much they already weigh. The less you currently weigh, the more you'll need to gain and the more you weigh, the less you'll need to gain. Those who are underweight will need to gain between 28 and 40 lbs, while those who are overweight should only gain between 15 to 25 lbs. If you're pregnant with more than one baby, expect these numbers to be higher.

- **Weight is not just fat**

Weight gain is crucial for your pregnancy and that's because you're not just gaining fat. In fact, if a woman gains 35 lbs during pregnancy, only 5 to 9 lbs will consist of fat stores. Increased breast tissue, blood supply, uterus growth, amniotic fluid, the placenta, and of course, the baby itself all take up that extra weight. Putting on less weight could mean giving your baby less of what it needs to be completely healthy – so don't try to put on less than your recommended weight.

- **Weight gain isn't consistent**

You won't gain weight steadily throughout your pregnancy. You'll go many weeks remaining at a consistent weight but you'll also see times, usually in the second trimester, where weight gain happens very rapidly. And later in the third trimester, as you approach your due date, all weight gain will come to a halt.

- **Safe exercise can keep excess fat off**

Not only will it help with weight gain, but it can also relieve aches and pains during the latter part of pregnancy. The important thing is that exercise isn't too strenuous. The perfect way to stay active is by making walking a part of your routine. Doctors recommend starting with at least ten minutes of walking a day and adding ten minutes every month. And remember, the walking you do while running errands counts too! If you enjoyed jogging before you were pregnant, feel free to continue doing this.

What About Stretch Marks?

When skin stretches due to rapid weight gain, this can result in stretch marks. Over the course of pregnancy, women may get stretch marks on their belly, breasts, thighs, upper arms, and sometimes even on their buttocks. Fresh stretch marks often appear slightly red or purple but as they get older, they'll fade to a white or silver color.

Unfortunately, there is no sure way to avoid stretch marks completely. Nine out of ten women get them to some degree during pregnancy. Genetics will also play a big role in determining whether you get stretch marks and their appearance. If your parents or grandparents developed stretch marks, you're more likely to as well.

Even if you're genetically predisposed to get stretch marks, there are steps you can take to lower your chances. The following practices have proven to help with minimizing and preventing stretch marks:

Get Enough Vitamin D

Studies have shown that low levels of vitamin D can increase the likelihood of getting stretch marks. To increase your levels of this important vitamin, consider eating foods fortified with vitamin D (many types of cereal, milk or yogurt) or getting more sun exposure.

Stay Moisturized

Stretch marks are far more likely to appear on dry skin – so to stave them off, make sure to keep your skin moisturized. Consider using brands such as Mederma, Earth Mama, or Bio-Oil which have all been known to help with existing stretch marks as well as prevention.

Stay Hydrated

Moisturizing on the outside is one thing, but increasing your water intake and moisture-levels inside can be far more beneficial for stretch mark prevention. When your body is fully hydrated, your skin softens and is, therefore, much less prone to developing stretch marks. Women with dry skin will find it a lot more difficult to avoid scarring from weight gain.

Get Lots of Vitamin C

Stretch marks or not, vitamin C is known to be highly beneficial in the pursuit of healthy skin. This is because vitamin C plays a crucial role in your body's production of collagen – an important protein responsible for your skin's elasticity. To boost your levels of vitamin C, eat more fruit and veg or consider taking a vitamin C supplement.

Control Your Pregnancy Weight

A mother should never limit her nutrient intake in pursuit of being smaller-sized, but mothers *can* limit the amount of food they eat. Focus on small but frequent meals, rich with all the nutrients you need. And when you can, try to stave off cravings for unhealthy food!

Treat Stretch Marks as Soon as They Appear

The sooner you treat stretch marks, the higher the likelihood of improving their appearance. Once you see purple or red marks forming, make sure to lather on a reliable stretch mark-control product or moisturizer. For the best luck, you'll need to treat the affected area daily even if you don't see results as fast as you want to. Even those who moisturize diligently can end up waiting a month to see big improvements.

5 Health-Boosting Supplements for Mom and Baby

As soon as you become pregnant, your body starts to demand more nutrients. This is true of macronutrients such as protein, fat, and carbohydrates, but it is especially true for micronutrients, which include vitamins and minerals. To make sure you're meeting this growing demand, it's recommended that women either commit to eating a nutrient-rich diet or at the very least, make supplements a part of their daily routine. If you're experiencing strong aversions to food or nausea during your pregnancy, you're going to want to keep a stock of these supplements so you're still getting the nutrients you need.

In addition to these supplements, make sure you talk to your doctor about the best prenatal vitamins for you to take. Your prenatal vitamins will cover a decent chunk of your nutrient requirements, but not everything. It's always best to see what your prenatal vitamins give you and what you need to get most of elsewhere.

Please note that all the supplements on this list have been deemed safe by medical health professionals. If you're considering taking a supplement that is not on this list, speak to a doctor before doing so.

Folic Acid

Recommended Amount: 600 mcg

Natural Sources: Asparagus, eggs, beets, avocado, spinach, broccoli.

Vitamin B9, commonly known as Folic Acid, is well-known for being vital to a growing baby's development and overall health. Numerous studies have shown that folic acid is directly responsible for reducing the risk of certain birth defects and abnormalities. Doctors even recommend a folate supplement for women trying to get pregnant, as intake before pregnancy brings even more benefits. Although it is possible, most women do not eat enough folate through their diet alone so a supplement can help greatly.

Vitamin D

Recommended Amount: 50 mcg

Natural Sources: sunlight, fatty fish such as salmon or mackerel, egg yolks, foods fortified with vitamin D including dairy and some cereals.

Vitamin D deficiency is, unfortunately, very common, not just in pregnant women but all people. In pregnancy, an inadequate intake of vitamin D has been linked to bone fractures, abnormal bone growth, preeclampsia, bacterial vaginosis, and rickets in newborns. Vitamin D is an essential nutrient for all pregnant women as it plays a prominent role in building your baby's bones and teeth. Unlike most other vitamin deficiencies, it is possible to be vitamin D deficient and display no obvious symptoms.

Iron

Recommended Amount: 27 mg

Natural Sources: oysters, clams, mussels, chicken or beef liver, spinach.

Your maternal blood volume will increase by 50% during pregnancy, so this means your need for iron will as well. Iron has proven to be crucial in the healthy development of both the fetus and the placenta.

Iron deficiency, or anemia, has been linked to a higher risk of infant anemia, preterm delivery and even depression for the mother-to-be. With iron, it's important that only the recommended intake is consumed and not more than that. Too much iron can induce vomiting, constipation, and many other unpleasant side effects.

Magnesium

Recommended Amount: 310 mg

Natural Sources: Dark chocolate, avocado, almonds, cashews, tofu, pumpkin seeds, flax seeds, spinach.

A woman's requirement for magnesium increases during pregnancy, and since it gets excreted in larger amounts through urine or vomiting (morning sickness), it is advised that mothers replenish their magnesium levels through their diet or supplementation. Studies have shown that a magnesium deficiency in pregnant women leads to a higher risk of preterm birth, preeclampsia, and fetal growth restriction. Sufficient levels, however, have been linked to reduced cramping while pregnant and, believe it or not, newborns with better sleep cycles!

Iodine

Recommended Amount: 260 mcg

Natural Sources: Cod, plain yogurt, cottage cheese, shrimp, eggs.

Our daily requirement for iodine is extremely tiny in comparison to other vitamins and minerals – but that tiny amount is very important. In pregnant women, iodine assists the thyroid in regulating hormones that control your heart rate, metabolism, and other functions. Mothers who do not get enough iodine significantly increase the risk of their baby being born with an underdeveloped thyroid. This can lead to a child with deafness, birth defects, learning disabilities, a low IQ, and much more. Since too much iodine can also pose serious risks, doctors recommend taking an iodine supplement with only 150 mcg and no more.

Before we dive into the first trimester, please keep in mind that everything in this chapter applies to the entire pregnancy. Make good habits part of your daily routine and eventually, both you and your baby will reap the benefits!

Chapter 2 - The First Trimester

Did you know the first trimester begins before you're even pregnant? Unknown to most, Day 1 is not the day of conception, but instead the first day of your last period before becoming pregnant. The first trimester lasts from this day until the end of week 12. When a woman discovers she is pregnant, she's usually five or six weeks into her pregnancy already. By this point, a heartbeat can usually be detected. Believe it or not, your baby grows the most rapidly in the first trimester than in any other trimester. More changes happen in such a short space of time than at any other point in your pregnancy. Curious about what these changes are? Here are some of the biggest developments of the first trimester:

- The fertilized egg has implanted itself into your womb – where it'll continue to grow for the next eight to nine months.

- The embryo will start dividing into three layers. The topmost layer will eventually form your baby's skin, eyes, and ears. The middle layer will become your baby's bones, kidneys, ligaments, and most of their reproductive system. And from the bottom layer, your baby's other organs such as the lungs and intestines will begin to develop.

- By the time week 12 rolls around, your baby's muscles and bones have formed, as well as all the organs of their body. It has a distinguishable human form and can now officially be called a fetus.

As these big developments take place, a mother's body starts to experience a lot of new feelings. You're likely going through some of these already. Rest assured, it's all part of the process that is the formation of life.

10 Common Symptoms of the First Trimester & How to Manage Them

You'll start feeling pregnant long before you start looking pregnant. It may be the early days but the first trimester is still fraught with its own set of symptoms. When you don't know what to expect, it can be difficult to distinguish between what's normal and what isn't. Not every mother will experience the symptoms on this list – in fact, you may even find that it varies with each pregnancy you have. If you're experiencing any of the following symptoms, know that it's completely normal and most mothers will tick off at least a box or two. And best of all, there is some degree of relief available.

1. Morning Sickness

There isn't just one cause for morning sickness, but it's largely due to rising hormone levels. Unfortunately, the term 'morning sickness' is rather misleading. Pregnancy-related nausea and vomiting can hit you at any time of the day, typically starting after week 6. As awful as you may feel, doctors do not advise skipping meals; in fact, you may find yourself feeling even worse on an empty stomach. Instead, just limit yourself to small meals, drink plenty of fluids, and sip on some stomach-soothing ginger tea. If nausea persists, consider getting some acupressure wristbands. Thankfully, morning sickness tends to subside by the second trimester.

2. Fatigue

Your body is making a lot of adjustments and changes to accommodate a baby, and naturally, this can result in extreme tiredness. Sometimes the best thing to do is to just let yourself relax and lay down, as you please. Now's the time for self-care. Curl up on the sofa and read, watch TV, or do whatever it is you enjoy doing in your spare time. If you're frustrated with being sedentary all the time, consider adding energy-boosting foods to your diet. Some of these include sweet potatoes, spinach, and oatmeal. And while you're at it, make sure you're drinking enough water as dehydration can add to pregnancy fatigue.

3. Constipation

It's normal to have more trouble than usual with bowel movements while pregnant. If you're not exercising or drinking enough water, this can contribute to the problem. It's also common knowledge that certain prenatal vitamins can make constipation even worse. If the problem persists after hydrating and exercising more often, you may want to speak to your doctor about switching to different vitamins.

4. Aversions to Certain Foods

Due to hormonal changes, you're likely to feel completely repulsed by certain foods. This is usually linked to feelings of morning sickness. Some of the foods you'll feel averse to may include spicy food, meat (especially red), garlic, milk and any others that give out a strong smell. The only way to manage this one is to be kind to yourself – if a certain food makes you feel sick, don't force yourself to eat it. You can find those nutrients in other foods. Have fun at the grocery store and pick out many different options for yourself. Once you're home, sort the ones that make you feel sick from the ones you can stand or actually like.

5. Food Cravings

And then you have the very opposite of food aversions – cravings! The feeling that you just gotta have it and you gotta have it *now*. For the most part, there's no harm in indulging your food cravings. However, it may become a problem if you're craving very specific foods all the time or your cravings are extremely unhealthy. Believe it or not, 30% of women report of craving non-food items such as soap or chalk. If you're experiencing non-food cravings, please do not satisfy these urges!

Before satisfying a craving, try drinking a tall glass of water first. It's actually surprisingly common to mistake thirst for hunger. Make sure you're not dehydrated before you rush to indulge. A second way to keep cravings at bay is by adding more protein to your diet. Studies have found a link between more protein at breakfast and the number of cravings throughout the day.

6. Frequent Urination

The need to frequently urinate can crop up as early as week 4 into your pregnancy – before you even know you're pregnant! Your kidneys need to become more efficient at getting rid of waste during your pregnancy, so this is an annoying side effect of extra blood flow going to your kidneys and pelvic area. Unfortunately, this symptom only becomes more extreme as pregnancy continues. Soon, your uterus will begin growing and so will your baby, increasing the amount of pressure on your bladder. There's no way to stop this altogether and it is highly advised that pregnant women do not minimize their water intake to attempt to control it. To avoid making it worse, limit your intake of coffee, tea, and soft drinks, which only increase the urgent need to urinate.

7. Tender and Swollen Breasts

Your body is preparing to provide nourishment to a baby and when the baby arrives, it'll need sustenance from your breasts. To prepare for this, your breasts will begin to grow and change – and this can result in skin that is tender or swollen. This starts in the first trimester and will continue throughout your entire pregnancy. If you're still using your pre-pregnancy bras, this may be exacerbating the issue. Give your breasts the support they need and consider purchasing a high-quality maternity bra. This may not solve the issue altogether but will definitely provide some relief.

8. Mood Swings

If you're feeling moody, restless, easily irritated, or just more down than usual, rest assured that it's completely normal. Depression and mood swings are common when your hormones are on overdrive. A key way to manage these symptoms is by making sure you're sleeping enough and eating a nutritious diet. Since your energy levels are already low, it's important you continue to recharge so your emotional wellbeing doesn't suffer. And always remember to make time for fun. If you're working while you're pregnant, make sure there's always time each day to devote to an activity that brings you joy.

9. Heartburn

During pregnancy, a woman produces higher levels of the hormone progesterone. This hormone has a soothing effect on certain muscles, including the ring of muscle in the esophagus. Unfortunately, when this muscle relaxes, it has a harder time keeping acids in your stomach, leading to acid reflux and – you guessed it – heartburn. To lower your chances of heartburn, doctors recommend avoiding spicy or acidic foods, eating smaller but more frequent meals, and waiting at least an hour before laying down after a meal. And to soothe heartburn, a glass of honey and milk or a small cup of yogurt can do wonders.

10. Skin Changes

You've likely heard of the 'pregnancy glow' where your cheeks get rosy and your entire complexion just seems a little brighter. Mothers-to-be tend to get the pregnancy glow in the first trimester, fairly early on. But unfortunately, not everyone will see positive changes. Some women will experience more oil than usual and this may even result in acne and breakouts. If you were prone to breakouts during your period, chances are that pregnancy will make you break out too. Thankfully, these skin changes are temporary and will subside once your hormones go back to normal. Whatever you do, steer clear of skin products with salicylic acid or vitamin A (retinol) unless you speak to a doctor first as these ingredients are known to affect pregnancy.

When to Call Your Doctor

You probably won't experience any big problems during your pregnancy, but it's always important to stay informed. If any of the following symptoms apply to you, call your doctor for additional help. It could indicate a more serious problem.

Heavy Vaginal Bleeding

Spotting is very common for pregnant women, but heavy bleeding is usually a cause for concern especially if there is any cramping or abdominal pain. In the early days, there is still a chance for a miscarriage or an ectopic pregnancy. Heavy bleeding can often be a signifier of one of these unfortunate complications.

Vaginal Discharge and Itching

It's completely normal to have some vaginal discharge during pregnancy – but look out for unusual discharge that's accompanied by itching. This could be a symptom of a sexually transmitted disease (STD). These are usually treatable but they can sometimes have negative effects on your pregnancy. If it's possible you have an STD, reach out to a doctor right away so it doesn't affect your baby.

Severe Nausea or Vomiting

Some level of morning sickness is an expected part of pregnancy, but if any of the following applies to you, contact your doctor.

- You vomit more than three times a day on most days.
- You've gone 12 hours without keeping down any liquid.
- You've thrown up blood, even if it's a small amount.

Urination with a Burning Sensation

Urinary Tract Infections (UTIs) are very common in pregnancy. While it's usually nothing to worry about, it becomes a more serious matter when you're pregnant. If left untreated, a UTI can cause a kidney infection, which has the potential to trigger a preterm birth or lead to a low birth-weight baby. Antibiotics from a doctor can easily solve the problem of a UTI, so it's essential mothers-to-be seek treatment for a fully preventable complication.

A High Fever

There are many potential causes for a high fever in pregnancy – while some of them are no cause for concern, it's important to rule out more serious causes. At its worst, it could be an infection, which may result in developmental complications in your growing baby. Even if you feel strongly that it's just a normal fever, doctors do not advise self-medicating since some pain-relieving medicines are dangerous during pregnancy. Be safe at any sign of a fever and call your doctor.

5 Ways Your Body Will Change in the First Trimester

As your body prepared to make a home for a baby, it will see a range of new changes and developments. While many of these will happen later on in the pregnancy, a good deal of changes will start as early as the first trimester.

1. Your Breasts

As your mammary glands increase in size, your breasts will swell to prepare for breastfeeding. Your areolas (the colored areas around your nipples) will also get darker and larger. For some women, the sweat glands in this area can also become larger, resulting in tiny, white bumps.

2. Vaginal Discharge

Pregnant women tend to get more vaginal discharge than they're used to. Normal discharge is milky with a thin consistency. Some women are more comfortable when they wear a small pad.

3. Hair Thickening

Many pregnant women report of thick and shiny hair that looks even healthier than it did before pregnancy. Unfortunately, this can also be accompanied by more hair growth on other areas of the body, such as the face, stomach, and sometimes even the back. You can thank rising estrogen levels for this!

4. Brittle Nails

Another side effect of higher estrogen levels is brittle nails. Many mothers find their nails are softer and more prone to splitting. It isn't all estrogen's fault, however; many experts think that increased blood flow in the toes and fingers could also be the culprit.

5. Bigger Feet

Don't worry, this doesn't happen to all women who get pregnant! Due to an increase in growth hormones, many mothers-to-be get bigger and sometimes flatter feet. It'll happen gradually over the course of your pregnancy. Believe it or not, some women have grown a whole shoe size!

What is a Doula & How Can They Help?

A birth doula is a trained professional whose primary job is to provide physical and emotional support to mothers over the course of their entire pregnancy. Although they can be hired at any time, including at the last minute, it's recommended that mothers hire a doula as early as possible, to allow more time for getting comfortable with your doula.

If you choose to hire a doula, she will assist you with the following:

- Breathing techniques, labor positions, and soothing through massage or other relaxation methods on the day of labor and delivery.

- Coaching and supporting the father (or other birth partner) so that they, too, can provide the best support for the new mother.

- Emotional support through the ups and downs of pregnancy, until the very end and perhaps even beyond.

- Letting you know whether you're in labor and when it's time to go to the hospital.

- Creating a more comforting environment for labor and delivery, e.g. with soft music, dim lights, candles, etc.

- Helping you to and from the bathroom (when needed) and making sure you've eaten and drunk enough on the day of delivery.

The contributions of a doula go far and wide, and many women claim they could never have done it without the help of one. This said, it's important to remember that a doula does not provide medical advice. Her assistance does not replace help from a doctor.

What Are the Benefits of Hiring a Doula?

Doulas have proven to have the following benefits on a mom and her pregnancy and childbirth experience:

- Significantly reduced anxiety.

- Decreases the time spent in labor by 25%.

- Less likely to need an epidural or other pain relief medication.

- Chances of needing a C-section lowered by 50%.

- Higher chances of breastfeeding success.

- A better bonding experience with the new baby.

- An overall more positive childbirth experience.

How Much Does a Doula Cost?

The cost of a doula varies widely and for some people, they may even be partially or completely covered by your health insurance provider. If you're paying out of pocket, expect a doula to cost between $800 and $2500.

Is a Doula Right for You?

As remarkable as a doula can be, not every mother feels she is the right fit for one – and that's totally okay! It all depends on your personality. Some women dislike the idea of someone they don't know being present during intimate moments. Keep in mind your doula will be there for some of your most difficult days. She will be getting up close and personal with you because that's the best way she can help. While most women find a doula's support empowering, others feel they get enough support from elsewhere.

If you have a very supportive and hands-on family with lots of pregnancy and childbirth experience, a doula may not be necessary. And if you take a long time to feel comfortable around a person you don't know well, your personality type may not be the right fit. But unless you fall into any of these categories, I've found that doulas are always incredible help. Many families stay in touch with their doulas because they gain a friend after the many months spent together. If you can afford it, consider a doula.

How Can I Find a Doula?

There are many ways to find the doula of your dreams. Try searching online directories such as:

- DONA International
- Birthing From Within
- Childbirth and Postpartum Professional Association (CAPPA)
- Doula Match

Choose the doula that suits your needs (in this case, you'd need a childbirth doula) and interview as many candidates as you can. You'll be spending a lot of time with this person so make sure that it's someone you feel comfortable with! And of course, always ensure that they have the right training and certifications. When you find the doula you're meant for, you'll get a good gut feeling!

For many moms, the first trimester is the most difficult – especially if you have some intense symptoms. Thankfully, some easier days are ahead. As moms transition into their next trimester, they find a lot of relief from their difficult symptoms.

Chapter 3 - The Second Trimester

Welcome to the second trimester! You're about halfway through the journey and you're probably incredibly relieved to reach this milestone. Many difficulties of the first trimester like morning sickness and fatigue will ease away in the second trimester. It's likely that you're feeling more energetic than you did and your breasts may even feel less tender. If you aren't feeling these positive developments yet, hold on! They'll get there soon enough.

In the first trimester, you will have gained little or no weight (unless you were very skinny) but this will change in the second trimester. Your belly will expand significantly in these next few months and you'll finally start to look pregnant. Since it's a period of rapid growth, this is when stretch marks are most likely to appear. You'll have more need for maternity clothes during this time, so make sure you're well-stocked with pregnancy wear that offers you comfort and support.

There's a lot happening inside your belly. Over the second trimester, these changes among many others begin to take effect:

- Your baby's organs are fully developed now.

- Your baby can hear! His or her first sounds will be the sound of your voice, the beating of your heart, the grumbling of your belly, and all the other fascinating noises of the human body.

- You'll finally be able to feel your baby moving around. This is more common later on in the second trimester.

Pelvic Floor Exercises that All Mothers Must Know

Now that you're more settled into your pregnancy, it's time to work on strengthening your pelvic floor muscles. This is a completely optional practice and will have no bearing whatsoever on your baby – but mothers who strengthen their pelvic floor are always relieved they did. This practice is just for the benefit of mom!

During pregnancy and birth, a woman's pelvic floor is stretched beyond its usual limits. These muscles are responsible for keeping the bladder closed and controlling urine that goes out or stays in. When the pelvic floor muscles become weakened, a woman is more likely to leak urine accidentally, especially while sneezing, coughing, or straining in some way. Since these muscles also help keep the anus closed, there may even be less control over breaking wind.

Unfortunately, pelvic floor muscles do not get stronger on their own. To avoid the embarrassing moments listed, women must make the effort to strengthen their pelvic muscles and better yet, make these exercises part of their routine. Some of these exercises may feel difficult to do at first but with practice, you'll get the hang of them. Just as other muscles in your body can get stronger, so can your pelvic floor.

Isolating the Pelvic Floor Muscles

This is an essential first step and one that is best tried while sitting on the toilet. While urinating, stop the flow midstream. The muscles you've just activated are your pelvic floor muscles. See if you can stop yourself from urinating for two seconds and then continue emptying your bladder as normal. It's important to note that this is not a pelvic floor exercise; this is just a way to help beginners identify the pelvic floor muscles. It is not recommended to habitually stop urination midstream. If you find yourself tightening your buttocks while trying to isolate these muscles, then you haven't yet succeeded. It's okay – just keep trying!

Once you've identified your pelvic floor muscles, you're ready to start exercising them. If you're a beginner, it may be best to empty your bladder completely first. And a word of caution: stick to the reps listed and do not over-exercise – or you may find this practice backfiring.

- **Exercise #1**

This beginner's exercise can be performed anywhere, at any time. Tighten the muscles in your pelvic floor and hold them for ten seconds. Then, relax the muscles for ten seconds. Perform ten repetitions, three to five times a day.

- **Exercise #2**

Get into a sitting position and imagine that you're sitting on a marble. Next, tighten the muscles in your pelvic floor as if you're pulling that marble upwards. Imagine lifting the marble with your pelvic floor alone. Hold the marble for three seconds and then release it for three seconds. Perform ten to fifteen repetitions, three times a day.

- **Exercise #3**

Instead of holding the marble for three seconds, try only holding it for one second. To do this faster-paced exercise, pull the imaginary marble upwards quickly, lift it, and immediately release. Perform these fast contractions as well as the slower ones a few times a day.

5 Ways to Start Bonding With Your Baby

Although you can start bonding with your baby at any time, the second trimester is an especially wonderful time to do it. As I mentioned at the beginning of this chapter, your baby can now hear you. This opens up many more ways to bond with your little one. Here are some ways you can start bonding now:

1. **Sing to Your Bump**

Your baby knows your voice extremely well by now. Since its the main voice he or she hears, it has become a very soothing sound and vibration. Sing a song or melody you love and send that positivity inside your belly. Your baby will enjoy being soothed in this way.

2. **Talk to Your Baby**

If you're not much of a singer, then don't stress. Your baby likes your voice regardless of whether it's in tune or not. To bond through the sound of your voice, try talking directly to your baby instead. Tell him or her how excited you are to meet or what the best parts of your day were.

3. **Respond to Kicks**

This method of bonding can be very fun. The next time your baby kicks, rub or massage the spot where you felt the kick. Some mothers even find that the baby will kick again. A back-and-forth can ensue – almost like a conversation!

4. **Self-Care**

Taking care of your mind and body used to just mean taking care of *you*. With a baby on board, however, you're taking care of two people. During acts of self-care, you'll instantly feel more calm and at peace – and this means your baby will get the message too. The next time you take a warm bath or get massaged, both you and your baby can bond through the soothing and relaxing sensations.

5. Prenatal Yoga

Not only will prenatal yoga allow you to get good exercise, but it's also a great opportunity to feel close to your little bump. As you pay attention to your breath and keep an open awareness of the being inside you, your baby will instantly feel at peace. Overall, prenatal yoga has some very positive effects on a mother-to-be's wellbeing.

Watch Out For These Signs of Preeclampsia

During a woman's first pregnancy, her risk of developing preeclampsia is at its highest. This risk is raised even higher if she is obese, very young or older than 40, carrying more than one baby, conceived through in vitro fertilization or if she has a family history of preeclampsia

The major risk of preeclampsia is that it eventually leads to a life-threatening complication, such as organ damage, placental abruption or eclampsia – a very serious condition where both mom and baby are at risk of death. Unfortunately, the only way to cure preeclampsia is by delivering the baby and oftentimes, preeclampsia strikes when a baby is too young to be delivered. At this point, the new mother is left with a difficult decision: risk two lives and carry the baby to term or abort the pregnancy. Since preeclampsia can start as soon as 20 weeks into a pregnancy, it's important that you pay attention to your body's changes in the second trimester.

The symptoms of preeclampsia are:

- High blood pressure in pregnant women who have never before had high blood pressure.

- Sudden swelling in the face, eyes or hands – though keep in mind that ankle and feet swelling is completely normal during pregnancy.

- Rapid weight gain, especially over a few days.

- Severe headaches.

- Vision changes such as blurry vision, temporary loss of vision or sensitivity to light.

- Reduced urination or no urination at all.

- Excessive nausea and vomiting.

- Abdominal pain, especially if it occurs in the upper right side.

- Severe shortness of breath.

Your routine prenatal visits will keep track of potential preeclampsia signs. But since many of these symptoms can come on suddenly, it's essential that you seek help as soon as they arise. Do not take chances with preeclampsia symptoms.

The Best Ways to Exercise in the Second Trimester

You're starting to expand and you're likely wondering how you can get some safe exercise. The good news is that you can still do most of the activities you were doing in the first trimester. As long as exercise isn't strenuous and doesn't come with a fall risk, it's probably safe to do. Here are some of the most popular methods of exercise among pregnant women in the second trimester:

1. **Swimming**

No matter the trimester, whether it's the early days or late in the third trimester, swimming is one of the best ways for a pregnant woman to exercise. Not only is it incredibly safe (with absolutely zero fall-risk) and low-impact but many women find it soothing on their aches and pains. If you'd like to incorporate swimming into your exercise routine, just make sure to avoid strokes that require you to twist your middle-section and abdomen around. Go for 15-30 minute sessions (depending on how much you swam before you became pregnant) at least three times a week. If you're a more experienced swimmer, it is safe to do it daily.

2. **Yoga**

Remember when I said yoga is a great way to bond with your baby? It's also just a great form of exercise for all preggo moms. Yoga allows mom to breathe and stretch out her sore muscles, reducing the aches and pains of pregnancy. It can also teach her breathing techniques that may be beneficial later on during labor. To stay 100% safe, doctors advise sticking to gentle positions and avoiding poses like the Tree or Warrior which make it more possible for mom to fall over. And steer clear of poses that require you to lie on your back or twist at the waist. Hot yoga is also strongly discouraged during pregnancy.

3. Walking

Walking is always safe during pregnancy, so rest assured that if all other exercises fail, a good and leisurely walk will do the trick. Experts even recommend trying to engage the arms as you walk; this can build strength and flexibility in your upper body. For the best exercise, walk at a faster pace to get your heart rate a little higher. As long as you're free from a fall-risk (no difficult hiking!), this is completely safe for mom and baby. This is also true for women who are heavily pregnant.

4. Light Jogging

Light jogging and running are only recommended if you did this before you got pregnant. If you used to jog before, feel free to try a toned-down version of your previous routine. The most important thing is that you pay attention to your body and immediately stop running if you feel any back or joint pain. Fall-risk is also a concern with this exercise, so experts recommend only running on a treadmill with reliable safety features or a flat, unbroken sidewalk. Women who are not used to jogging or running are not advised to start doing it now.

10 Fun Ideas for the Second Trimester

If I had to choose the trimester I enjoy the most, it's by far the second trimester. With so many difficult pregnancy symptoms out of the way, you can finally embrace and enjoy being pregnant. No more nausea means food is wonderful again. No more fatigue means you can finally get some stuff done and feel good about it. You're at that perfect middle point. Here are some of my favorite fun second-trimester activities.

1. **Have a Gender Reveal Party**

Most women find out the gender of their baby in the second trimester. Know what this means? It's the perfect time for a gender reveal party! Gather your friends and family to celebrate the unveiling of your baby's gender. Many people enjoy filming the reactions of both parents to learning this exciting new detail about their baby. If you're interested in throwing a gender reveal party, there are a number of fun reveal ideas! Consider a gender reveal cake, balloon pop, confetti, or if you're feeling wild, fireworks!

2. **Announce Your Pregnancy Publicly**

Announcing a pregnancy in the first trimester is always risky since the chance of a miscarriage happening is highest at that point. Once you're in the second trimester, however, you can finally safely make the announcement! Whether you're holding a gender reveal party or not, you can have fun with your announcement to your wider group of friends on family. An adorable social media post or a beautiful card are some ideas you can use. What an exciting time!

3. **Go on a Babymoon**

If you've ever wanted a second honeymoon, now's your chance! The second trimester is a great time to enjoy your final vacation before having a kid. By the time the third trimester rolls around, you'll find that most airlines won't let you fly internationally, so now's the time to get your international travel fix. If you don't have the time or money for a big vacation, then why not see a different part of the country or have a staycation? Whatever form it takes, you and your partner should absolutely enjoy your last months as a child-free couple.

4. **Go on a Shopping Spree for Maternity Clothes**

You're going to see some significant weight gain in the second trimester and that means it's time for some new clothes. Go maternity shopping by yourself or with some other pregnant friends. And for the best selection, look online. Treat yourself to new clothes that make you feel fantastic about your new body. Many new moms prefer more fitted clothes to baggy clothes; this allows them to embrace their new curves, making them instantly feel more sexy. You deserve to feel good, first-time mom!

5. Buy Some Lingerie to Restart the Fire in the Bedroom

If you're feeling a little more sensual than usual, you can thank your fluctuating hormones! Enjoy these feelings and bring your partner into the mix to enjoy them too. If you're so inclined, throw in some new lingerie the next time you go maternity clothes shopping. You'll get a lot bigger in the third trimester so now's the time to get lingerie you can still wear after you're pregnant!

6. Have a Maternity Photoshoot

Flaunt your new body and feel beautiful! Maternity photoshoots are not about vanity; it's about commemorating a beautiful time in your life. As a first-time mom, how wonderful would it be to make memories if your experience in the form of gorgeous photographs? The second trimester is perfect as you look pregnant enough for a maternity shoot but you're not big enough to start getting self-conscious. Browse online for a good maternity photographer or ask for referrals from friends. It may sound like a wild idea but many mothers deeply cherish these photos! Feel free to get your partner involved as well.

7. Incorporate Gentle Exercise into your Routine

Now that you're in the second trimester, you've likely gotten your energy back. Without the fatigue to hold you back, it's a great time to start getting into gentle exercise. Take a look at the previous section and find an exercise method that you like best! If you weren't very fit before you got pregnant, take it easy as you're not any fitter now that you're expecting. Always listen to your body!

8. Decorate and Furnish the Nursery

When your baby arrives, you'll want to have the nursery completely ready. If you're planning on having it painted, it's especially important that there aren't any lingering paint fumes. Get the essentials out of the way in the second trimester while you have the energy to decorate and furnish. The bigger you get, the less time you're going to want to spend on your feet. If paint and chemicals need to be handled, get your partner to take over this job and make sure you aren't inhaling any dangerous fumes.

9. Interview More Doulas

If you haven't decided on a doula or are making last minute decisions about having one, now's the time to get serious about the search. Doulas can be hired at any time but the earlier you have one on board, the more help they can offer. Interview more doula candidates and have one decided on before your second trimester ends. It's totally possible to have fun with this! Many doulas end up forming a friendship with the family, so you can even try to see this as interviewing a potential new family friend. Get to know these candidates and laugh with them. If you're still struggling to find a childbirth doula, search for them online or ask other mothers you know for referrals.

10. Take a Childbirth Class

It's not too late to take a childbirth class. If you didn't attend one in your first trimester, consider doing it now. Mothers who make the time to take these classes are always glad they did – and some birthing centers even require you to take them! The information you'll glean is invaluable. Another bonus? You'll meet other first-time moms, the perfect allies on this crazy ride! Connecting with other first-time moms is one of the best things you can do for yourself. When both your babies are born, you can empower each other and help each other learn. When you're done with childbirth class, consider taking others on breastfeeding or newborn care.

Chapter 4 - The Third Trimester

You're finally in the home stretch of your pregnancy the third and last trimester. This trimester is easily the most exciting as it ends with the ultimate reward: bringing your baby out into the world and getting to hold him or her in your arms. Keep in mind that, although you may have a due date set, there's a chance your baby will arrive sooner than you expect. It's important that you recognize the signs you're going into labor, as soon as they arise. But before we get into that, here's a quick rundown on how your baby is continuing to develop in these final months:

- Your baby's eyelashes have formed and he or she is now capable of opening their eyelids.

- It's finally happened! Your baby can kick! He or she can also stretch and gently grasp.

- Hair has grown – and if you have thick hair genes, it's possible your baby is starting to develop a fantastic head of hair.

- What a little cutie – your baby's skin is now smooth and taking on a chubby appearance.

To sum up, your baby is finally starting to resemble a full-on tiny human. Your body is putting the finishing touches on the child you'll soon hold in your arms. In the meantime, however, there's a lot to do to prepare for his or her arrival.

Every First-Time Mom's To-Do List for the Third Trimester

1. **Finish Your Baby's Nursery**

As soon as your little bundle comes home from the hospital, you'll want to have his or her nursery ready to be slept in. This means you'll need a cot. If you plan on painting the nursery, get this done as soon as possible so that your baby does not have to be exposed to the smell of paint – which can be harmful if exposure lasts for more than a brief moment.

2. Prepare Everything Your Baby Will Need

When your baby comes, the last thing you'll want to do is rush to the store. Both you and your partner will want to enjoy every second of being with your newborn – any interruption would be extremely annoying! The third trimester is the perfect time to stock up on your baby's essentials so you don't need to run out for them later. You'll need diapers, blankets, newborn onesies, and much more. Get the full list in the following chapter.

3. Read as Much as You Can

This new chapter of your life is like no other chapter you've known before. This is why it's strongly encouraged for all mothers to fully inform themselves about how to properly care for a child. Thankfully for all mothers, there's a lot of information out there, easily accessible to all. In fact, by reading this book, you're already making strides towards being a fully prepared mom! Still, you shouldn't stop at one book. Absorb as much information as you can from as many sources as possible.

4. Make Self-Care a Priority

You're carrying a child and your body deserves all the love it can get. Do everything you can to avoid strain and needless stress. Actively practice self-care. Pamper yourself with a prenatal massage at a great spa and when you're feeling tired, sit in bed and enjoy your favorite TV show. Do whatever makes you feel great. And keep in mind that self-care sometimes means doing something that is good for you, even if you don't really feel like doing it. Sure, treat yourself to a chocolate milkshake if it brings you joy, but more often than not, care for yourself by seeking out more nutritious options. To operate from a mindset of self-care, consider what your body really needs at that moment to create the best emotional environment for your baby.

5. **Start a Baby Registry**

There's no reason you should buy all the essentials yourself! Baby registries allow parents-to-be to list all items they need when their baby arrives. This, then, allows friends and family to give these items as gifts. Consider making your own baby registry on Amazon, Bed Bath & Beyond or Target.

6. **Stock Your Freezer**

With a new baby around, new parents tend to have a lot less energy for their regular cook-ups. Still, that's no excuse to neglect your hungry bellies and nutrient intake. You're going to need those calories! The third trimester is the perfect time to stock your freezer with microwavable meals or anything that doesn't require more than two steps to prepare. Pack as much in as you can. Neither you nor your partner will want to head out to the grocery store with a new little baby. If you prefer home-cooked meals, then an alternative is to cook your own meals to freeze for later.

7. **Clean the House**

This may seem like a strange to-do activity, but trust me, you'll be glad you did it when your baby comes. A surprising number of moms wish they'd cleaned up their home before their baby's arrival. Once the little bundle comes, there's simply no time or energy to deal with a messy house. Whether you do it with a partner or hire someone else to do it, try and get your home spic-and-span and mess-free before your big day.

8. Rest!

Once mothers enter the third trimester, it gets a little more difficult to sleep. No matter what you do, you just can't seem to get as comfortable as you used to. Nevertheless, it's important that moms get as much rest as they can. With childbirth on the horizon and exhausting days with a newborn baby looming, now's the time to try and get some much needed rest. It won't just be you and your partner for long! Make the most of the time you have to stay horizontal for as long as you like.

9. Decide Whether to Breast or Bottle-feed

To breastfeed or formula-feed – that is the question. Or at least, it is *one of* the questions of the third trimester. If you haven't decided yet, it's about time you do so. Why? Because very soon you'll need to start shopping to prepare for your new baby. And breastfeeding and bottle-feeding moms need slightly different equipment. If you're still feeling indecisive, let's examine the advantages of both options.

Breastfeeding vs. Formula Feeding

Breast

- When it comes to the nutrition factor, breast really is best. Mothers pass antibodies through their breast milk, meaning that their child is more resistant to certain illnesses and infections, such as meningitis and ear infections.

- Breast milk is easier to digest than other options. This means there's a much lower chance of your baby getting gassy or constipated.

- Breastfeeding is the least expensive option. You will need to buy formula but breast milk is, as you know, completely free. The money you spend on formula will quickly add up but breastfed babies just not you, a breast pump, bottles, and very few other supplies.

- Studies have shown there is some link between breastfeeding and babies with high levels of intelligence, i.e. cognitive function.

- Breastfeeding is also great for mothers. There is evidence that breastfeeding mothers have a lower risk of getting breast cancer, diabetes, ovarian cancer and more.

- Experts aren't so sure why but there appears to be a connection between breastfed babies and a reduced risk for Sudden Infant Death Syndrome (SIDS). Babies who are breastfed for at least six months are much less likely to die in their sleep.

- When breastfeeding happens regularly, it can burn up to 500 calories per day. If you're interested in shedding weight quickly after pregnancy, breastfeeding can help greatly.

Formula

- Formula feeding is far more convenient for mothers. Formula can be fed at any time and there is no need to take time out of your schedule to pump milk. This means your partner can feed the baby at any time, without needing help from you first.

- Babies don't digest formula as quickly as they digest breast milk, so there will be far more time between formula-feeds as opposed to breastfeeds. In other words, your baby will not need to be fed as often.

- There's no need to restrict your diet in any way. Babies that consume breast milk are very affected by what their mother eats and drinks, but with a formula-fed baby, mom can have whatever she likes. Foods and drinks that mothers should avoid while breastfeeding include hot spices, citrus fruits, alcohol, and anything with a high amount of caffeine. For the full list, see Chapter 8.

Tackling Third-Trimester Insomnia

As I mentioned previously, insomnia in the third trimester is not uncommon, especially for first-time moms. A number of factors contribute to this inability to sleep, from frequent urination and body pains to simply feeling huge and not being able to get comfortable. All new moms need their precious sleep; here are some helpful tips for fighting pregnancy insomnia.

1. **Invest in a high-quality pregnancy pillow.** You can find these in most maternity stores and they will work wonders for your sleep routine. Pregnancy pillows provide the perfect amount of support for mom so she can finally get in a comfortable position. Doctors actually recommend that pregnant women sleep on their left side after week 20, as this allows more blood flow to get to your baby. A pregnancy pillow is designed to make this position more comfortable.

2. **Make light exercise part of your routine.** As much as moms hate to hear it at this point in their pregnancy, a little daily exercise can help greatly. It may be difficult but try to get up and about at least once a day – it'll make you sleepier at night. Just try not to do it too close to your bedtime or you'll be buzzing with energy.

3. **Wear loose and comfortable nightwear.** Steer clear of tight-fitting clothing and stick to light materials like cotton that allow your body to breathe. And if sleeping in the nude is the most comfortable for you, then why not? Do whatever you need to get sleep, first-time mom.

4. **Use as many pillows as you need.** This is especially important if you can't afford a pregnancy pillow. Get all the cushions and pillows in your home together (though you should probably leave at least one for your partner!) and experiment with as many arrangements and configurations as you can. Remember that sleeping on your left side is best for your baby right now. To mimic the support of a pregnancy pillow, try putting a cushion under your belly and between your knees.

5. **Sleep wherever you get comfortable.** If it's on your living room sofa or in an armchair, go for it. It doesn't have to be in your bed. Wherever you find yourself drifting off, allow yourself to just fall asleep. Sleep is hard to come by so take it whenever it comes.

6. **Fully hydrate by the early evening.** This way, you'll cut down on the number of times you need to go to the bathroom in the middle of the night and you'll still get all the water you

need. Start hydrating as soon as you get up and stop drinking water when the evening rolls in.

7. **Get help from your doctor.** Thing is, some sleep medications and aids are perfectly fine to have while pregnant – but you should never go on them without telling your doctor first. If no other methods work, feel free to ask your doctor for more serious relief. He or she will be able to prescribe a sleep aid that is safe for your baby and exactly what you need.

Labor Signals & What They Mean

Natural birth or C-section, it's vital that every mother-to-be recognizes when they're going into labor. Even if your due date isn't for a few more weeks, it's always possible to have a premature baby. Each mother is going to have a slightly different experience during the weeks or days before labor sets in, but here are some of the many signals you're likely to experience and what they mean.

- **Your Baby Has 'Dropped'**

When the baby starts to sink lower into the pelvis, this is a key sign that the body is preparing for labor. But hold up, this doesn't necessarily mean that you're on the verge. A baby drop can happen as early as a month before labor.

- **An Increase in Back Pain and Cramping**

As your body prepared for birth, your joints and muscles with shift around and stretch. Unfortunately, this means more back pain and cramping for mom. While this is certainly a sign that labor is coming somewhat soon, there is no need to rush to the hospital. This signal means labor is as far as a month away and soon as a few days away.

- **Bloody Show**

In late pregnancy, thick vaginal discharge mixed with mucus and blood gets released by the vagina. This pink-hued discharge is called the 'bloody show' and it's a sign that the cervix is preparing for labor. The bloody show can indicate that labor is anywhere from a few weeks to a few hours away. If it's accompanied by other signals on this last, then labor may be close.

- **Your Water Breaks**

The water break is one of the last signs of labor a woman will experience. In other words, if it happens to you, you're most certainly in labor and your baby is on the way soon. Movies have misled people into thinking a public water break is common – but in reality, a premature break rarely happens. For most women, the water break happens well into labor and sometimes even moments before the baby actually emerges.

- **Contractions**

During labor, intense contractions are known to precede the time of delivery, but false-alarm contractions do exist. And this can confuse matters for many women. Braxton Hicks contractions are not labor contractions. Instead, they signal that the body is getting ready or warming up. There are many ways to tell Braxton Hicks contractions from Labor contractions, the most notable difference being that real contractions get more intense and closer together. When this is felt, you're most definitely in labor!

Braxton Hicks Contractions vs. Labor Contractions

Even though we've covered one way to distinguish between a false-alarm and real labor contraction, there are other signifiers too. No one wants to drag themselves all the way to the hospital just to be told to go home again – so let's make sure you understand these key differences! Here's how to know whether you're truly in labor or not:

Intensity

Braxton Hicks - These contractions are usually mild in intensity, without much variation in strength. Many women have also experienced them as strong to start with but weaker over time.

Labor - Contractions that indicate real labor have nowhere to go but up in intensity. They only get stronger and stronger over time.

Pain

Braxton Hicks - Pain is located on the front of your body, in your lower abdomen.

Labor - Pain exists in both the abdomen and the back. Some women even report that pain is *more* extreme in the back of the body. This is because the whole body prepares for real labor, not just one side.

Timing

Braxton Hicks - There is no discernible pattern between contractions. They come on seemingly at random with no specific regularity. They do not become more frequent.

Labor - Contractions come regularly and get closer together.

Adjustments

Braxton Hicks - Contractions stop or weaken with a change of position such as sitting, laying down, or walking.

Labor - It doesn't matter what you do, labor contractions still continue.

How Do You Induce Labor Safely and Naturally?

For labor to happen, two hormones are needed – prostaglandins and oxytocin. These two hormones trigger contractions and help to expand the cervix so that a baby can emerge. The key to inducing labor mostly revolves around trying to stimulate these hormones and therefore, labor. While many 'old wives tales' exist around the use of certain herbs, studies have not yet been performed to prove their efficiency or safety. Furthermore, many people suggest castor oil as a way to induce labor. I can confirm this method *does work*, but I highly discourage using it as it is also a laxative. Mothers who use castor oil end up going into labor dehydrated and with diarrhea. Do not make labor harder on yourself!

It is also extremely important to note that no one should try to induce labor unless they are due or past their due date. Inducing labor before your time should not be done unless a doctor gives you the OK.

- **Nipple Stimulation**

Let's make one thing clear: this type of nipple stimulation is not sexual at all! For this method to be successful, stimulation needs to mimic the suckling of a baby. Doing this will release oxytocin in the brain and may result in your uterus contracting, therefore beginning the process of labor.

- **Membrane Sweeping or Stripping**

If you're desperate, membrane sweeping is always an option – though it must be performed by your doctor. Using a gloved finger, your doctor will reach inside you to separate the amniotic sac from an area just inside the cervix. This releases prostaglandins and stimulates contractions to induce labor. Expect some discomfort during this procedure.

- **Having Sex**

It's important to note that sex doesn't always work at inducing labor. Still, there's a chance it might. Not only does sex release prostaglandins but male ejaculate also contains it. If the man ejaculates inside the vagina, it's possible the cervix will wake up and start contracting.

- **Eating Dates**

This method will not induce labor instantly, but if you start a few weeks before pregnancy, you may never have to induce labor. Studies have shown that eating 60-80 grams of dates per day in late pregnancy can reduce the need for induction and improve labor overall. Women who ate dates regularly decreased the length of the first stage of labor to almost half the time of women who didn't.

Chapter 5 - Preparing for the Big Day

When the big day arrives, the last thing you want to be is unprepared. No matter the type of birth you're having, there are a variety of ways you can and should make yourself more comfortable. Just a little prep can go a long way. Unprepared first-time mothers find themselves far more stressed and uncomfortable when the big moment arises – so avoid this, now that you have the choice. Follow these simple steps and you'll have everything you need to devote your full attention to you and your baby.

Pack These 13 Essentials in Your Hospital Bag

There's a possibility your little one will come knocking sooner than you think – so start packing your hospital bag just in case! Mothers who pack at the last minute (or allow someone to do it for them!) have admitted to ending up with a lot of useless stuff they didn't really need and without the stuff they really *did* need. The birth of your first child will be such a special time and the last thing you want is to be inconvenienced by something you could have prepared for.

1. **Your Daily Toiletries**

What essential toiletries are part of your morning and nighttime routine? Pack travel-sized versions in your bag. A stay at the hospital is no reason to neglect your self-care; in fact, it's a bigger reason to make it a priority. Bring your toothbrush, toothpaste, deodorant, and whatever else makes you feel cozy and at home. For efficiency and ease, consider getting some cleansing facial wipes instead of your usual face wash.

2. **Hair Ties and Clips**

The last thing you want is your hair getting in your face while you're giving birth. Pack hair ties and/or clips to keep your hair pulled back so you can focus on the big task without any minor annoyances.

3. Snacks and Drinks

This one is easily overlooked. It's not that food and drink aren't available where you'll be, it's more about the fact that mom and dad often want to stay together. Swept up in the special moment, it isn't uncommon for dad to opt for staying with mom instead of going off wandering for food. Without snacks readily available, many new parents can forget it's been several hours since their last meal.

4. Lip Balm

Have something that keeps your lips moisturized. Many mothers find their lips get chapped as they endure the intense hard work of labor. Keep those lips hydrated!

5. Comfortable Shoes

Ideally, these should be easy to slip on and off as you may want to do some walking around the hospital. Avoid all shoes that require you to bend over and/or strain in any way to get them on.

6. Pillows

Every hospital will provide pillows but don't expect them to be as comfortable as the ones you have at home. To ensure you're as comfortable as possible during this special but physically challenging time, bring your favorite pillow from home. Your partner may also want to bring a pillow as well.

7. A Dark-Colored Bathrobe or Dressing Gown

Whether it's in early labor or the postnatal ward, you're definitely going to be up and about in the hospital at some point. Make sure you're warm and comfortable by bringing something to wear over your hospital clothes. If you're worried about stains showing, pack something that's dark-colored.

8. Entertainment

Since mom will be preoccupied most of the time, this is more of a 'need' for dad. Pack something that can provide entertainment for many hours. This could be a book, a magazine, a music player, or something else. Whatever it is, make sure that it doesn't stress out or overwhelm mom!

9. Loose Clothes

Bring comfortable clothes, not just for the hospital but for your first ride home with your baby. It's important that you're not wearing anything too tight as you'll feel tender after delivery. Pack clothes that open easily at the front. This way, you'll be able to feed your baby with no difficulty as soon as the need arises.

10. Postpartum Underwear

Many first time moms get the mistaken impression that the hospital will supply them with proper underwear. Those who don't get *that* mistaken impression instead wrongly assume that it's fine to bring the underwear they wear normally. For starters, do *not* bring underwear that you would be upset to ruin. You will bleed heavily after giving birth and you'll need something that is up to the task. Get high-quality postpartum underwear that provides support, protection, and comfort.

11. Eyeglasses

This only applies to you if you wear them, of course. New mothers tend to not want to deal with their contact lenses when they're giving birth at a hospital. Since labor can take a while and it's possible you may be in and out of sleep, glasses tend to be the easier option. This may be down to personal preference. But if you're having a C-section, keep in mind you will be asked to remove your contact lenses beforehand.

12. Everything You Need to Be Photo-Ready

For some moms, this may mean nothing at all – but others might like to bring some mascara or powder to look a little less worn out in photos. This is completely up to mom and her preferences. Your partner and family members are likely excited to document the special day so bring any clothes or makeup you need to feel wonderful.

13. Massage Oil or Lotion

During the hours before labor or even after birth, many moms find massage incredibly soothing. Kick this up a notch by bringing a massage oil or lotion with a fragrance you find pleasant.

22 New-Baby & First-Time Mom Necessities

Of course, preparation is not just about the hospital visit and childbirth. It's also about that other special day – the day you get to bring your little one home. As soon as you get home, you'll need to have everything ready. Aside from a fully finished nursery with a crib or bassinet, you'll also need your child's smaller necessities. Take note of the following essentials; if you don't get them through your baby registry, get them yourself as soon as you can.

1. Diapers

Your newborn is gonna be one heck of a pooper – there's no way to avoid it! Needless to say, you're going to need diapers and a lot of them. Every mom can take their pick of disposable or cloth diapers.

- Disposable

Pros: *Most convenient option, more absorbent, less time-consuming.*

Disposable diapers are still a wildly popular option and it's no wonder why. The toss-when-you're-done approach is very convenient and requires no extra cleaning from mom or dad. But be prepared to spend more money in the long run – on average, parents who use disposables spend upwards of $2000 over two years. Not only this but the total amount of diapers used will create a lot of non-biodegradable waste for the environment. If you prefer the ease of disposable diapers, consider getting eco-friendly products from companies like *Honest*.

- Cloth

Pros: *Much cheaper in the long run, adjustable, kinder to sensitive skin, irritation less likely, reusable, eco-friendly.*

Over recent years, cloth diapers have become more widely used. Not only is it a money-saving option but cloth diapers today are far more effective than they used to be, thanks to innovation around eco-friendly baby products. To safeguard against potential skin irritation, cloth diapers are the way to go since absorbent chemicals in disposables can cause bad skin reactions for some babies. However, all parents who choose this route should keep in mind that cloth diapers require a lot more effort and time. Once your batch of diapers has been soiled, they'll need to be deep cleaned.

2. One-Piece Baby Clothes

Save the cute two-pieces for when your baby is a tiny bit older. To start off, focus on onesies or one-piece clothing that is easy to put on and take off. Since babies are extremely messy, you'll need to change your baby's clothes many times a day – keep this in mind when choosing clothes! Ideally, these garments should snap open at the bottom so you can do a diaper change with minimal hassle.

3. Mittens

If the onesies you've purchased don't cover your newborns hands, then some mittens will serve your newborn well. These are to ensure they don't scratch themselves with their little nails. Just two pairs should do the trick.

4. Baby Wipes

Try to get baby wipes that are suitable for more sensitive skin. Although your baby may not need a sensitive solution, it is always best to be safe with a newborn. These wipes will be used to clean your baby's bottom half during changing. On these sensitive areas, more care is needed.

5. Receiving Blankets

These multi-purpose blankets can be used for a myriad of things and they'll be your best friends in the months to come. Receiving blankets are soft, made of thin cotton, and usually come in a pack of three or four. Not only will these blankets provide your baby with comfort and warmth, but they also make great burping cloths, playmats, and feeding blankets for if you want more privacy during public breastfeedings.

6. Burp Cloths

As the name suggests, burp cloths are for covering clothes and wiping up spills, in the event that your baby spits up. And believe me, it will happen a lot. Receiving blankets can make handy substitute burp cloths but traditional burp cloths are much smaller and easier to carry around. While that extra surface area can be nice, it's not always entirely necessary.

7. Swaddling Blankets

To keep your baby comfortable and fully supported, you'll want to tuck him or her into a swaddling blanket. Again, a receiving cloth can be used as one, but real swaddling blankets are larger in size, more stretchy, and oftentimes, specially designed so that mom and dad can swaddle their baby with minimal hassle.

8. A Baby Carrier

You're going to need an easy, comfortable way to carry your baby around with you. This is where a baby carrier comes in. This way, your little one can snuggle in close while you get around to do what you need to do. A good carrier offers your baby secure, safe and comfortable support. In the early days, a baby carrier is the best way to travel with your baby as it promotes intimacy and skin-to-skin contact. If you have a big baby or suffer from back problems, you may find a carrier uncomfortable – in which case you may need to pass on carrier duties to your partner.

9. Baby Bottles with Nipples

You'll need baby bottles whether you're breastfeeding or bottle-feeding. If you're feeding your baby breastmilk, you'll still need a way to feed your baby expressed milk so he or she can be fed without you around. These days, most parents prefer to use glass bottles to avoid the chemicals in plastic passing into the milk.

10. Changing Pad

Most parents designate an area in the room to change their baby's diaper. This changing station is usually made up of a changing pad on a solid, sturdy surface. Keep in mind that you'll be using this station multiple times a day, so it's important that it isn't wobbly, is in an area that gets enough light, and doesn't require mom or dad to crouch over in an uncomfortable position. Some parents also like to have a back-up changing pad in case the main one gets soiled.

11. A Diaper Genie or Pail

You're going to need a proper place to store dirty diapers between trash runs. Regular trash cans don't always do a great job at masking the bad odors – and this is where a diaper genie comes in. A genie or pail is capable of storing a load of dirty diapers without letting the bad smells waft into the room. If you have a big house, a diaper genie may not be absolutely necessary, but if your home is a tighter fit, you're going to want to keep that diaper smell out of the other rooms.

12. Car Seat

You're going to need a car seat as soon as you get into the car with your baby to head home from the hospital. For a newborn baby, it is advised that you purchase a rear-facing car seat. Until the age of two years-old, your baby should *not* use a forward-facing car seat.

13. Stroller

While a baby carrier pretty much always suffices for taking your baby wherever you need to go, you're eventually going to crave the freedom of a stroller – especially for taking your baby outdoors. And once your baby starts getting heavy, a stroller becomes an absolute must-have. Unlike a carrier, a stroller allows a baby to lay flat on his or her back and sleep comfortably. And once your baby ages, they can easily interact with the world while remaining comfortable. One of the other great things about a stroller is that it also gives mom a place to store baby essentials while on-the-go.

14. A Baby Bathtub

Many mothers survive just fine without a baby bathtub, but they make things a lot more convenient when bathing your baby. These days, baby bathtubs come with all kinds of hi-tech features, including temperature indicators. Feel free to purchase whatever makes the most sense for your budget. The most essential feature is the space it provides for your newborn to get wet, but not too submerged. Moms who opt out of the baby bathtub choose to just get in the big bathtub with their newborn in their lap. Or another alternative, using the sink. If you don't have a lot of space in your home, these two alternatives may be the best choice. Whatever you do – baby bathtub or not – do not get a bathtub ring as these pose more dangers than they prevent.

15. A Nursing Bra

When your milk comes in, your breasts are going to get much bigger. This means none of your current bras are going to be very helpful – including your pregnancy bras. To ensure you get the most comfort and support for your breasts, get fitted for a nursing bra. Ideally, you should do this as close to your expected due date as possible and no earlier than a month before. You are unlikely to be in the mood after your baby comes, so doing this beforehand is best.

For Breastfeeding

16. A Breast Pump

If you plan on breastfeeding, a breast pump is a core necessity. This allows you to express and store milk in advance so your baby can be fed even if you're asleep or away. If you find yourself engorged or with an oversupply of milk, a breast pump will be your best friend.

17. Containers or Bags for Milk Storage

After expressing milk, you're going to need a place to store it until it's needed. Ideally, it should be in something that is designed to store breast milk. There are many options for this and it all comes down to personal preference. Moms can take their pick of glass containers, breast milk trays, storage bags, or plastic milk bottles.

18. Nipple Cream or Lanolin Ointment

Believe me, your nipples are going to get sore. While there's no sure way to prevent it entirely if you're breastfeeding, you can take measures to avoid cracked and dry nipples. Applying cream or ointment to your nipples everyday can work wonders.

19. Breast Pads

When breastfeeding a baby, it isn't uncommon for the other breast (the one that's not feeding your baby) to also let out milk. As you'd expect, this can lead to a little and sometimes a lot of leaking. Some moms naturally leak more than others and it may have to do with their supply. Even when you're not breastfeeding, you'll likely experience leaking, especially once your baby starts sleeping longer hours and your body hasn't adjusted to the new schedule. And this is where breast or nursing pads come in to save the day. They prevent milk from leaking through your clothes. Mothers that don't intend to breastfeed also find breast pads helpful sometimes, as it's possible to experience some leaking before milk production dries up.

For Formula Feeding:

20. Formula

This one is a given! If you plan on formula-feeding your baby, make sure you have a large stock of all the formula you need for the next few to several weeks. It's important that the formula you buy is suitable for your newborn. The three types of formula are ready-to-use, powdered, or concentrated liquid. Talk to your doctor to determine the right kind of formula for your baby.

For Postpartum Healing

21. Maxi Pads

If you're planning on a vaginal birth, stock up on some maxi pads. You're going to be bleeding a lot after giving birth; make sure you're underwear and clothing are fully protected with these new mom essentials. You'll be using these for several weeks after giving birth and believe me, tampons will not do. If you're a waste-conscious person and you'd prefer to not use disposable products, know that there are plenty of reusable cloth maxi pads as well. Many moms find these even more comfortable than disposable pads.

22. A Tummy Splint

After pregnancy, many women experience abdominal separation. This is when the left and right stomach muscles separate slightly, resulting in tummy fat that looks disjointed from the rest of the stomach. This isn't just an aesthetic concern, it can also cause constipation, lower back pain, and at its most extreme, a hernia.

Abdominal separation is very common and happens to about two-thirds of pregnant women. Unfortunately, sit-ups can make the issue worse and while time can heal most of the problem, many moms are still left with a little pooch. The tummy splint is the easiest and safest way to minimize the problem after birth. This compression wrap applies light pressure so that mom's body has support and just the right amount of 'push' inwards. Even if abdominal separation isn't a huge concern for you, many moms find a compression wrap very comforting.

How to Start Creating a Birth Plan

On the day of your child's birth, you're probably not going to feel like making any big decisions. This is where the birth plan comes in. Having a birth plan prepared means your decisions and wishes about your baby's delivery are documented ahead of time. When your baby comes knocking, this means all your preferences are clearly outlined – so you can just focus on birthing your little bundle.

Keep in mind that sometimes unpredictable circumstances strike during birth, so there's always a possibility doctors will insist on a different course of action. And you, yourself, may want to make these changes. In any case, it is always helpful to create a birth plan. This step is completely optional, but many moms like having the chance to discuss and think through these decisions ahead of time. This is what you should include in your birth plan:

- **List the basics**

These include your name, contact information, and your doctor's name. If you know which hospital you'll be delivering at, include the name of this hospital too.

- **Name all attendants**

Who of your friends and family would you like to be present in the delivery room? Having this in your birth plan will ensure they're all allowed in during your big moment.

- **Atmosphere preferences**

Think of the environment that you'd most like to give birth in. What do you find calming or soothing? Would you like the lights dimmed or any type of music playing in the background? Are there any items from home that you need beside you to give you strength?

- **Your labor preferences**

Would you like to be photographed or filmed? Would you like to walk around freely? Birthing equipment may be available, such as a birthing stool or chair; include whether you would like anything like this. If you like the idea of being in a tub for labor and delivery, include this in your plan as well. And if you'd prefer to opt out of an episiotomy (snipping of the perineum for easier delivery), say so and be prepared to discuss this with your doctor.

- **Pain management preferences**

When the intensity of labor sets in, what are your preferences around the use of an epidural? What about other pain medications? If you're fine with the use of an epidural or other pain relief, would you like it as soon as possible or would you like to wait and see if you can do without it first? If you don't want any of the above pain medications, are there any alternatives you'd prefer?

- **Delivery preferences**

Would you like the opportunity to watch your baby emerge with a mirror? Many mothers even want to touch their baby's head as it crowns. If you have preferences around whether to have an episiotomy when necessary or to allow natural tearing, mention this. When your baby is out, would you like the father to cut the umbilical cord? If you're having a C-section, would you like the drape removed so you can watch your baby being lifted out of you? Do you want everyone else in the room to be silent so that your voice is the first thing your baby hears? It's possible that you may also have an IV or catheter inserted, so if you want to steer clear of this, include this.

For clarity's sake, it's always best if the birth plan is less than a page long and easy to read. Once you're done, share your birth plan with your partner and your doctor. Their input may be helpful before the plan is finalized.

Chapter 6 - Childbirth & Labor

At last, the time has come! The big day has arrived and everything you've prepared for in your childbirth class stands before you. Hopefully, your hospital bag is fully packed by now – if it isn't, get your partner or family member to gather what you'll need most (pillows, hair ties, and snacks!) and accept they may need to come back later. If it's your first birth, you're likely having it at the hospital either via planned or unplanned C-section, or natural birth. If you have a doula and she's not yet with you, it's time to let her know that your time is finally here.

By now, you, your partner, your doctor, and your doula (if you have one) should be well aware of the decisions laid out in your birth plan. Everyone will be trying their best to honor your wishes, but stay flexible. Unexpected things can happen which makes it difficult to honor very specific preferences; just know that whatever course of action is made, it will be in the best interest of you and your baby.

When it comes to childbirth, a good rule of thumb is to always expect the unexpected. No two births are exactly the same, even from the same mother. This said, there are many things to keep in mind on this big day. It's possible that not all of it will apply to you, but it's always helpful to prepare for the unexpected the best you can.

10 Less-Known Things You Should Know About Vaginal Childbirth & Labor

Everyone knows vaginal childbirth is challenging and painful, but what else? So much happens during labor – stuff you'd never know about unless you'd gone through it! – and all pregnant women should have the complete picture.

1. **Your doctor may not be with you until the very end, and sometimes, not even then.** Despite your many doctor visits, he or she won't really be needed until delivery takes place. Since midwives and other professionals are fully equipped and skilled to handle labor, there's no need for the doctor during this part of the process. The doctor may slip in and out to check in on you, but do not expect more attention than that. It's also possible that your doctor won't even deliver your baby, especially if he or she has partners at the facility.

2. **It's possible you'll get sent home, even if your contractions are real labor contractions.** Even though contractions definitely signify that you're in labor, the reality is that labor can last days. Unless your contractions are very frequent, coming every five minutes or less, then there's a possibility you'll get turned away at the hospital and told to come back later.

3. **The pain might be far more tolerable than you think - or far worse.** There's absolutely no way to predict how painful your childbirth will be. Of course, all women should expect some pain, but I've known many women who were blessed with relatively easy labors and a baby out in under ten minutes. On the other hand, I've also known women who claimed childbirth was even worse than they thought. There's no sure way to know.

4. **You will probably poop in the middle of childbirth.** Many women are horrified to learn this fact, but unfortunately there's no way to ensure it doesn't happen. The reason behind this is simple: when you push out your baby, you engage the same muscles you use to have a bowel movement. In addition to this,

your baby creates a lot of pressure on the rectum and colon as it squeezes through the birth canal. It's absolutely essential that women do not become consumed by self-consciousness when this happens. Doctors are completely used to seeing this happen in the delivery room, as it happens to most women. What doctors do mind is that this self-consciousness can often prevent women from pushing properly, making everyone's job a lot more difficult. Just focus on delivering your baby and know there's no reason to worry about anything else.

5. **There's a possibility you'll throw up or be nauseous.** Not all moms experience this, but many do and it's completely normal. If you're using an epidural, which causes blood pressure to drop, this can bring on nausea or vomiting as it sets in. Though even if you aren't using an epidural, these side effects are still a possibility. While you're giving birth, many of your body's functions slow down or stop, including digestion. And if you have a lot of food in your stomach, it may need to come back up. If you'd like to minimize your risk of vomiting, stop eating and stick to water once you're in active labor. And in early labor, try to only eat light food.

6. **A lot of people will be there over the course of your labor and childbirth.** Although this depends heavily on the type of facility you'll be delivering at, for the most part, it takes more than two or three people to deliver a baby. If you're having your baby in a big hospital, expect to see many different faces over the course of labor and childbirth. Not only will you need a nurse or two, but you'll also need a midwife, the doctor, various assistants, and if your hospital is a teaching hospital, then possibly even medical residents. Don't be alarmed when

you see more than a few new faces. It's all completely normal and everyone is just there to help.

7. **Your doctor may need to open you up wider.** To help get your baby out, your doctor may think it is necessary to give you an episiotomy. This is when an incision is made along your perineum (the skin between your vagina and anus) so your baby can be delivered easier. Doctors usually do this for a good reason but in many cases, it is possible to opt out of it. Speak to your doctor about this beforehand, if you'd like to avoid an episiotomy. But also know that you may want one – it can move things along when you're running out of steam!

8. **You'll deliver far more than just a baby.** Don't worry, this isn't as scary as this sounds. After giving birth, mom is going to need to expel a few things that she no longer needs in her body, namely the placenta (also known as the afterbirth) and lots of blood and tissue. New moms are always alarmed by how much blood comes out of their body after birth; expect it and don't be nervous.

9. **Overwhelming happiness may not be your first emotion after giving birth.** After a physically and emotionally exhausting birth, and labor which may have lasted hours or days, it's normal for mom to be emotionally shut down. This is a normal response while extremely exhausted and it's important that everyone lets mom rest. And mom, too, should not be ashamed that she isn't jumping for joy after such a physically draining experience. Just give mom some time to recharge and she'll wake up with the incredible joy that everyone else is feeling as well.

10. Childbirth is difficult on partners too. Of course, it won't be nearly as much of a challenge as it is for mom – but that doesn't mean it isn't a challenge for dad or other birth partners! It isn't uncommon for nurses to take someone out of the delivery room because it's too upsetting to watch their loved one in so much pain. If this happens, do not fault your partner for having this reaction. Many partners do.

4 Things to Do for a Safer C-Section

There's no need to worry about your C-section. It's true that it comes with more risks than a vaginal birth, but this is true of all surgeries. Complications from cesareans are rare and women generally have a lot of control when it comes to avoiding these complications. Many new mothers are interested in the precautions they can take before and after their C-section. Here's what you can do to ensure you steer clear of the risks of a C-section.

1. **Wash yourself with antibacterial soap before surgery.** Doing this ensures that there is less bacteria in the area where you will be cut, therefore reducing your risk for infection – one of the biggest risks associated with C-sections.

2. **Do not shave your pubic hair yourself before surgery.** If it needs to be removed, it will be trimmed carefully by surgical staff. Shaving can increase your risk of infection.

3. **Keep warm the best you can.** Getting cold before or during a C-section can raise your risk of infection very slightly. Make sure you're snug and warm in all the blankets you need.

4. **Walk as soon as you can after surgery.** Yes, you will be sore, but walking shortly after surgery gets your blood moving again

– and this is essential for reducing the risk of blood clots. Whatever you do, don't overdo physical activity. Just make sure you get some time on your feet to start the healing process.

The Lowdown on Epidural Anesthesia

When it comes to pain relief during childbirth, epidural anesthesia is the most prominently used. Not only is it administered for c-sections and vaginal deliveries, but it also relieves pain for a number of other surgeries and body pain from a prolapsed disc.

How is an Epidural Administered?

The epidural is injected with a needle into the lower back, specifically in the area around the spinal nerves. A local anesthesia is given in this same area prior to the epidural, so mothers do not feel too much pain from the second round of anesthetic. Epidurals numb the body below the place of injection, so mom's birthing pains are lessened significantly and yet she can still stay awake during childbirth or c-section. It takes roughly 15-20 minutes for the anesthetic to take effect. Since the bottom half of the body is numb, a catheter is usually inserted until the effects of the epidural wear off.

Why Should You Get an Epidural?

An epidural is completely optional for vaginal births. Many women claim they absolutely need it and others cope just fine without one. The biggest and most obvious advantage to the epidural is, of course, having a far more painless or, in some cases, *completely* painless delivery. Many women find the pain of childbirth unbearable and if labor was difficult as well, some mothers just can't handle anymore. Free of pain, many mothers find that they are completely clear-headed during labor.

Why Shouldn't You Get an Epidural?

There are a few reasons why some moms opt out of the epidural. Some women do not like the sound of the side effects, which can include headaches, nausea, urination during delivery and inability to control it for a short while afterwards, temporary nerve damage, and difficulty walking. Due to the lack of sensation in the lower half of the body, women under epidural anesthesia tend to also have a hard time pushing effectively during delivery. So even though birth becomes painless, an epidural can prolong the overall time of labor. After birth, the anesthetic still needs time to wear off, so mom won't be able to feel her legs for a short time after.

Like with most things, epidurals come with their own risks. There is always a small possibility (roughly 0.5%) that moms will develop a post-dural puncture headache – a severe headache that sets in anywhere from a day to a week after an epidural. The pain from this headache will become intense when upright in a seated or standing position but lessen when lying down. Accompanying the pain, there may also be nausea, vomiting, neck pain and an extreme sensitivity to light. Despite being painful, this is easily treated by a doctor.

Will an Epidural Affect the Baby?

Unfortunately, a lot more studies need to be done on this subject. There is some evidence to show that epidurals have a subtle effect on newborns, but this hasn't been explored in detail. What we do know is that epidurals do not harm a baby, as far as we know, and if there are any side effects, they are not serious. For example, some studies have shown that epidurals may lead to issues breastfeeding, namely with getting the baby to "latch on" to the breast – but this does no lasting damage to the baby.

7 Helpful Tricks for Pushing that Baby Out

1. **Push as if you're going to the bathroom, i.e. having a bowel movement.** This always throws first-time moms off! Naturally, they think that if they're trying to push a baby out and *not* go to the bathroom, they shouldn't be using those muscles. This is wrong! And this is why it's difficult to avoid having a bowel movement while giving birth. If it feels as if you're pooping, you're on the right track! Don't be embarrassed and just get it done.

2. **Use big focused pushes instead of smaller frantic ones.** Many first-time pushers try to conserve their energy and opt for light but frequent pushes. These will prove very ineffective and may just prolong the time spent in labor. Put focus and a lot of energy into every push! Frequent and intense pushes are far better than prolonged pushes.

3. **Don't strain or push with your upper body.** This won't impact your baby's birth but it may leave mom with facial bruising or bloodshot eyes. When mothers let out an intense push, they instinctively pull their upper body into it as well. To avoid bruising in the upper body, push only with your lower body and do not strain your face too hard.

4. **Don't be afraid to try a different position.** Most women give birth lying on their back but other positions have proven much more helpful for getting a baby out. If lying on your back isn't doing the trick, try squatting upright. This way, gravity can assist with birthing your baby.

5. **Keep breathing and do not hold your breath for longer than a few seconds.** When in intense pain, many people naturally start to hold their breath. Resist doing this when you're giving birth. Take deep breaths whenever you can and especially before each big push.

6. **Don't push until you feel like pushing.** Being in labor doesn't mean you're ready to push. You'll know when you are! And when the time comes...

7. **Push when you feel like pushing!** Your body knows when the right time is. In fact, pushing is more like an involuntary response and reflex. You'll have to try hard to not do it. If you know you're fully dilated and the urge comes, go for it.

The Best Positions for Pushing with an Epidural

Epidurals will make the pain of childbirth a lot more manageable. In some cases, it may eliminate the pain entirely. Unfortunately, along with the elimination of pain, an epidural can also numb or diminish urges to push. These urges are very helpful when it comes to getting a baby out as they basically tell mom when she should be pushing. When mom can't tell what's happening with her body, pushing the baby out becomes a lot more complicated. Thankfully, there are many birthing positions that may make it easier on mom and baby. If you're taking an epidural, keep these positions in mind:

- Lying on the side.

- Kneeling by or at the foot of the bed while leaning over.

- Squatting with support from others.

- Lying on the back with legs in stirrups or supports.

- Upright sitting position.

- Half-sitting with knees pulled towards you.

7 Little-Known Things about C-Sections

1. **You'll still feel your baby coming out.** It won't be painful in any way but you'll still be able to feel a vague tugging at your abdomen. If you've had other types of surgery before, it is not too different from that.

2. **The surgical team may seem unusually casual.** Even though this is your first birth, the surgical staff taking care of you have done this plenty of times before. Many first time moms are taken aback by the casual and laid-back chatter amongst the staff. Learn to see this as a positive thing! It means everything is going exactly as planned so you can just relax.

3. **If you want to watch your baby come out, you can.** Even if you haven't included this preference in your birth plan, you can still ask to have this arrangement on the day. Just make sure you're ready to see a lot of blood!

4. **Your partner may not be prepared to see you cut open.** It's customary for doctors to warn birth partners about what they might see – and most will advise just focusing on your face – but squeamish or not, partners sometimes can't resist the temptation to look. It's not the easiest sight to behold so be prepared to see your partner get a little pale!

5. **Doctors might strap you down.** This doesn't always happen but it isn't uncommon. Many mothers find this unusual but it's all to ensure the utmost safety. The last thing anyone wants is movement that makes surgery more difficult. The good news is you'll barely feel your arms and they may even unstrap you once your baby is out.

6. **The birth will be quick but the stitching up will take some time.** In fact, your baby will be out within the first ten minutes of the surgery starting. Stitching you up, however, can take up to 45 minutes. This said, many moms barely notice the time going by when they're getting sewn up. Why? Because they're just thrilled the baby is out!

7. **You'll be numb for quite some time.** Thanks to the pain medication, you won't feel it at all the first time you touch your C-section scar. It's also possible you won't feel a thing the first time your baby breastfeeds. This upsets some moms but there's no reason to be – trust me, you'll feel your baby breastfeeding *a lot* after this point. The most important thing is that you and your baby are healthy, and a long, beautiful journey lays ahead of you.

Chapter 7 - Postpartum Care

First-time mom, you are a pillar of strength. You've finally brought your baby into the world and now, no one underestimates the fortitude you clearly possess. The journey only continues. After the difficulties of pregnancy and childbirth, it's absolutely crucial that you get in the habit of taking care of yourself, as well as your baby. Being the strong mother you are, it'll come naturally to you to just power through no matter how you're feeling. While this is an admirable ability, this attitude shouldn't dictate your lifestyle from now on. Not only are you transitioning into a new big role, but your body is also healing.

To ensure you take care of yourself in the best way possible, here are some of the many things you can do to nourish your inner and outer well-being. Get used to listening to your body so you can better identify what you need at any given moment.

What Every Mother Needs to Do after Giving Birth

1. Get A Lot of Rest

Needless to say, mom is going to need to rest and recharge. This can be difficult when you have a newborn. You'll find that your baby wakes up every few hours, needing to be fed, so getting a solid 7-8 hours will be pretty much impossible. A good rule of thumb is to sleep whenever your baby sleeps. Even if sleep only lasts for an hour or two at a time, these hours add up and can really help.

2. Get Help from Loved Ones

Whether it's your partner, family, friends or all of the above, make sure you get all the help you need with household chores and other responsibilities. Ideally, everything in the home should be taken care of, leaving you to focus on feeding the baby and taking care of yourself, until you've had more time to recover.

3. Get Good Nutrition

So many nursing others end up neglecting their diet and nutrition because they are just so tired. This is where your loved ones come in. Get a family member or your partner to help you adhere to a healthy diet; this will aid you greatly on the road to recovery. According to lactation experts, it's best if mom eats whenever she is hungry – but ideally, she should be eating an overall balanced diet with the right amount of calories and fat. These include:

- Whole grains, such as whole wheat or oatmeal.

- Unpasteurized dairy products, such as milk or yogurt. If possible, stick to low-fat or fat-free options.

- Fruits in any form, including 100% fruit juice. Tired moms may find that juice or a smoothie is the best and easiest way to get their fill of fruit.

- Vegetables – ideally a variety of them, including leafy greens, legumes, orange, red, and starchy vegetables.

- Protein with less of an emphasis on meats, especially red meats. The best proteins for recovering new moms are beans, seeds, nuts, and fish. For other types of meat, make sure you're only consuming lean meat.

9 Completely Normal Long-Term & Short-Term Effects of Pregnancy and Childbirth

1. Hair Loss

Remember when pregnancy hormones gave you thick, lush hair? A drop in those hormones means you're going to experience the opposite. After giving birth, many moms go through a period of hair loss. But don't worry, this isn't forever. This shouldn't last for more than five months.

2. Hemorrhoids

There's going to be general soreness in your nether regions after birth; if you notice some of this pain coming from your anus, then there's a good chance that you have hemorrhoids. This swelling can make bowel movements even more difficult than they already are with an episiotomy wound or tearing. If your doctor hasn't already given you a stool softener, it's time to ask for one. If you'd like other forms of treatment, try an over-the-counter cream for hemorrhoids or wear pads that contain a numbing solution. Hemorrhoids are easily treated, so there's no need to fret about this one.

3. Incontinence

I warned you about this, didn't I? Pregnancy and childbirth can really pull a number on your pelvic floor muscles. When the muscles that control urination, bowel movements, and passing gas are stretched or injured, it can lead to some frustrating side effects. Most moms experience some level of stress incontinence, which is when a little urine leaks out while laughing, coughing, or sneezing. Incontinence tends to improve after a few weeks but it isn't uncommon to have some lasting effects. Hopefully, you've been practicing your pelvic floor exercises! If you haven't, try doing them now.

4. Contractions

While the worst contractions are long behind you, it's normal to experience some cramping after giving birth. These are called afterbirth pains and they'll be the most intense on the few days right after childbirth. These contractions are a natural result of your uterus returning to its regular prepregnancy size. After a few days, you can expect afterbirth pains to gradually fade away.

5. Constipation

In the days that follow childbirth, it is extremely common to have some constipation. This tends to be caused by anesthesia and pain-relieving medication given to you at the hospital. These can slow down the function of your bowels for a short period of time. Some mothers also find themselves constipated out of the fear and anxiety of hurting their perineum. Stay fully hydrated and eat fiber-rich foods to ease constipation. If you think it might be anxiety causing this problem, talk to your doctor about using a stool softener. Constipation generally isn't a real problem unless you've gone four days after birth without having a bowel movement. At that point, contact your doctor anyway.

6. Wider Hips

Many women discover their body shape has changed after giving birth. Namely, their hips seem slightly wider. While some of this is down to pregnancy weight gain that will subside after a few months, it isn't uncommon for a woman's shape to see some permanent changes. During pregnancy, a woman's pelvis bone structure changes to allow a baby to move smoothly through the birth canal. Not every woman will find that this change lingers on, but a significant number do.

7. Mood Changes

I'll say this now and remind you later: don't feel guilty about your mood swings! Many moms are under the mistaken impression that they'll pop out a baby and have impermeable joy. This is a total myth and it leads to a lot of needless shame for a mom that just needs a break. Yes, you'll feel happy but you'll also go through a rollercoaster of other emotions. It's a combination of hormones and the fact you're just exhausted after the last nine months. Don't be hard on yourself! We'll get more in-depth with this later on.

8. Lower Sex Drive

For the same reason the mood swings come, a lower sex drive is very common in postpregnancy. This is especially true for breastfeeding women whose estrogen levels plummet even more from feeding their baby. Most women claim it takes, on average, a year for their sex drive to return to its normal state. But some only feel these effects for a few months. These effects will vary from woman to woman, as with most changes.

9. Melasma

If you've noticed darkened patches of skin on your cheeks, forehead, and/or upper lip, then you have melasma – and you're not alone. Melasma is triggered by any change in hormones. 50-70% of pregnant women are affected by it and many find it lingers long after they give birth. Most signs of melasma fade after a year but you may find that some dark spots need further treatment. Before you seek out the high-strength skincare that is usually prescribed for melasma, wait until you're no longer breastfeeding your baby.

10. Darker Skin on the Areolas & Labia

As I mentioned in a previous chapter, a woman's areolas get darker and sometimes bigger during pregnancy. Some women find that their nipples and areolas remain this darker shade even after giving birth. This isn't the only thing that changes, however; the labia, too, can become a darker shade and you may even see this same darkening with moles.

How to Help the Body Heal from Birth

Every mother is sore and in pain after childbirth. Depending on the type of birth you had, you're likely aching in more places than one. C-section or vaginal birth, doctors recommend that you abstain from sex for a few to several weeks. Absolutely do not try to do it anyway or your body will pay the price.

Follow your doctor's instructions and there will be nothing to worry about. You're most definitely on the road to recovery already, but here are a few other things that you can do to speed up the healing process.

Caring for Your C-Section Scar

Your doctor or nurse should have given you some helpful instructions about how to care for your C-section scar. It all comes down to two things: clean and dry. Ideally, you should be cleaning it gently every day with a little bit of mild soap and water. After washing, pat the scar dry with a clean towel. Most doctors will tell you it is completely fine to apply some petroleum jelly or an antibiotic ointment to your scar. However, some doctors feel it's best to let it be after washing and drying, with no oil or ointment whatsoever. None of these practices will do harm to your scar so feel free to choose what feels right for you, or ask your doctor what his or her preferred approach is.

Whenever you can, let your scar air out; air can help skin injuries heal faster. In addition to this, try to wear loose clothing to avoid rubbing against your scar. Your doctor should have also mentioned this, but avoid all exercise, especially during the first several weeks.

If your scar shows signs of swelling or redness in the skin surrounding it, or starts oozing out any liquid, make sure to contact your doctor as soon as possible.

Caring for Your Perineum

The perineum tends to be one of the most sore areas after giving birth. Whether you had it cut during delivery or it tore naturally, you're likely eager for some relief. Using an ice pack on the area every few hours can work wonders – especially the day after giving birth. After urinating, take extra care to gently clean the area, as urine can irritate the cut or torn skin. Spray or lightly splash some warm water on the perineum to prevent irritation. Do this before and after urinating.

Improving Urinary or Fecal Incontinence

Hopefully, you've been doing the pelvic floor exercises in Chapter Three! These will have given you some strength against incontinence. If you weren't quite so diligent about it, that's okay! You can start doing them as soon as you feel you are well enough. These would take effect immediately, but if you stick with it, you'll see improvements soon enough.

Easing Painful or Sore Breasts

Aside from using lanolin ointment on your nipples, make sure to also let your breasts breathe after each feeding session. Being exposed to cool air can have a soothing effect on the skin. Some mothers find that using a warm compress or heating pad on sore breasts can really help a lot.

Soothing General Achiness 'Down There'

If the pain gets too uncomfortable, the use of painkillers is always an option, especially acetaminophen can help greatly with pain in the perineum. Other soothing methods include taking a sitz bath and using a heating pad. Many mothers also swear by witch hazel pads, which can be used in conjunction with an ice pack to ease pain in the vagina and/or postpartum hemorrhoids.

Everything You Need to Know About Postpartum Depression

The birth of a baby brings incredible joy into the lives of two lucky parents. It is entirely common, however, to feel a range of other emotions. With joy, there may also be fear and anxiety about being a good enough carer or parent. And mothers may even feel the 'baby blues' starting as soon as a couple of days after delivery. These feelings are very normal and for many mothers, the blues can disappear in just a couple of weeks. When the baby blues last for an extended period of time, however, this is called postpartum depression. The symptoms of postpartum depression include:

- A pervasive feeling that you can't bond with your baby.

- Complete depletion of energy.

- Insomnia or oversleeping.
- Loss of appetite or overeating.
- Withdrawal from close friends and family.
- Excessive crying spells.
- Strong feelings of being an inadequate or bad mother.
- Restlessness and anxiety.
- Mood swings or general depression.
- Guilt, shame, and feelings of worthlessness.

If these symptoms persist for over two weeks, it is essential that new mothers seek out help for postpartum depression. This is especially important if symptoms cross the line into postpartum psychosis, marked most notably by feelings of confusion, delusions or hallucinations, obsessive thoughts that revolve around the baby, paranoia, and perhaps even thoughts or attempts to hurt oneself or the baby. The longer these conditions are left untreated, the longer they will continue. Help from a medical professional can allow new mothers to get back to a healthy frame of mind so they can enjoy their new role, as they deserve.

9 Soul-Soothing Self-Care Ideas for a First-Time Mom

1. Invite a Friend Over

If you're feeling up to it, why not invite a friend over? Once your newborn is a little more settled in and you've had time to recharge, getting some time with a friend whose company you love can be incredibly healing. While your baby is napping, you could have lunch together in your home and enjoy a movie or TV show. This is also a great time to make new friends with other first time moms. If you know anyone else who just had a baby, this may be the perfect time to form a bond.

2. Enjoy a Warm or Hot Bath

This self-care method isn't just soul-soothing, but it's also body-soothing, especially for sensitive areas that are sore. Feel free to also dim the lights, play music in the background, or light candles if you'd find it more comforting. You can do this at all hours of the day, whenever you need it the most. Do it between your baby's naps or simply ask your partner to take over for a while. Since you're probably tired, just make sure you don't fall asleep in the tub!

3. Pamper Yourself with a Massage or Manicure

You deserve to pamper yourself, new mom! Many new mothers feel guilty when they take time away from their baby to get pampered – but this guilt needs to stop. As long as you're not doing this excessively, you're giving yourself exactly what you need to be the best mom for your baby. Your body has gone through *a lot*; let yourself sit back so you can be taken care of for a moment. Whether it's a massage, a manicure, or a pedicure, do something that allows you to be still and be soothed.

4. Write in a Journal

Many new mothers love taking up journal-writing after they've had a baby. Even those who have never had a journal before. Documenting these early days can be very special and some moms even do it with the intention of sharing the journal with their child once they are old enough. Writing can center the soul and allow us to sit, breathe, and observe our everyday lives. If it feels like everything is changing and you haven't had time to yourself, the act of writing and recording can feel very anchoring. Deciding to not share this journal with anyone is fine too. Allow yourself to just feel what you're feeling and give yourself a safe space in a private journal. Find a time each day or every other day to write an entry in your journal, perhaps during one of your newborn's morning naps.

5. Reconnect with your Partner

With a new baby in the mix, many couples become overwhelmed and forget to take time to themselves. I don't just mean sitting down to watch TV in silence, but to actually talk and discuss how they're doing with the new changes in their lives. Remember what you did before the baby came along. Talk about what you used to talk about, make light of funny scenarios, and laugh together. Foster and nurture your connection, and you'll both find yourselves soul-soothed.

6. Dive Back Into an Old Hobby or Interest – or Find New Ones!

You may have a new baby but that doesn't mean you have to discard your hobbies and interests. In fact, it may be emotionally and mentally beneficial for you to get back into them. Studies have shown that when we regularly do something that takes us away from our usual train of thought, it triggers anti-oxidation in our body and combats stress. If you enjoy knitting, get back into it during the times you have to yourself. If you'd like to start sketching or blogging, now's not too late to start. Take your mind away, momentarily, and let your body destress.

7. Treat Yourself to Fun Soap, Lotion & Other Body Care

Now's the time to indulge in body care goodness. Whether it's LUSH, Bath & Body Works, or something else, treat yourself to products that make your body and skin feel amazing. The time you get to yourself in the shower counts as self-care; get all the fun flavors or flavors you can find and let yourself be soothed. If you have a C-section scar or any kind of stitching or tearing on your perineum, make sure to not rub any of these products directly on these areas.

8. Go on Frequent Walks

Walking is a great way for a new mother to get some exercise. It's safe for her recovering body, allows her to get some fresh air, and it can also improve her mood. Practice this healthy habit any way that works for you. You could take your baby out in his or her stroller, or you could ask your partner to watch your little one while you get some time alone to destress with a leisurely stroll. It may seem like too simple an act to make a difference, but you'll be surprised by how clear-headed and relaxed you can be from a walk. The best part is it doesn't have to take long and you can do it almost anywhere. Bring some music and headphones for an even more relaxing walk.

9. Take Care of the Basics

Sometimes the best self-care just requires doing the basics and doing them well. Many overwhelmed new moms are so exhausted they forget to do this. Eat nourishing food that you love, drink lots of water, use a lovely scented soap in the shower, and get some rest during your baby's naps. If you're not up for socializing, free yourself from those responsibilities. Just focus on taking care of yourself in the most basic but essential ways.

Chapter 8 - Your Newborn Baby

Holding your first baby in your arms is an unparalleled experience. To think you created this new life with your own body! What utter magic. You're going to have a marvelous time getting to know this tiny little human, but as you'll quickly realize, it's not all tickles and cuddles. Tiny humans need a lot of care and comfort. Since they don't have mom's strength yet, they're still very delicate and vulnerable. This chapter is packed with information on how to properly care for a newborn baby. As your baby gets older, your techniques and strategies will evolve as well – but for now, keep a close eye on these crucial details.

11 Things You Should Know About Newborn Babies

1. **It's normal for their skin to be dry.** After all, they were submerged in a wet womb before promptly hitting the air. The dryness can sometimes be alarming to new moms and dads, but it's actually completely harmless and there's nothing you need to do about it.

2. **If your newborn is fussy, try to mimic the conditions of the womb.** Consider how it felt for the baby to be snug inside your body and try to recreate that same environment. Try swaddling or gentle swinging, and accompany this by a light whooshing or shushing noise. You may even find that a warm bath has a soothing effect on your newborn.

3. **Make sponge baths the norm for the first couple of weeks** – or specifically, until the umbilical cord falls off. A sponge bath makes it easier to keep the umbilical cord dry, which is what it needs to fall off quickly.

4. **Expect some bleeding when the umbilical cord falls off.** Just think of it as a scab peeling off. Blood is normal and it's no reason to be alarmed.

5. **Newborns are near-sighted.** Just after birth, a newborn baby can only see about 8 to 12 inches in front of their faces. Everything beyond that is blurry and cannot be distinguished. As the months pass, your baby's sight will gradually get stronger. At three months old, shapes and colors will be much clearer.

6. **Don't fret if your baby loses a bit of weight.** A few days after giving birth, it isn't uncommon for babies to lose about five to ten percent of their body weight. This is not a sign that your baby is underfed. In fact, you'll discover your baby has gained more weight after a couple of weeks past birth.

7. **Breastfed babies have less smelly poop.** A strange fact but it's true! Just after birth, all babies have the same type of poop. But once you establish a feeding routine and decide on how you'll find your baby, the nature of their poop will quickly change. What does it depend on? Whether they're formula-fed or breastfed. Remarkably, the poop of breastfed babies does not stink at all.

8. **It's normal for newborns to have birthmarks.** These will appear pink or peach-colored on their face or neck. Some parents are even surprised to see these marks get more red when they're in distress. Roughly a third of babies will have these marks, so it's usually no cause for concern. But if you notice skin discoloration or strange bumps, it's always best to

speak to a doctor. Otherwise, these harmless pink marks tend to disappear within six months.

9. **Newborns can leak milk.** In fact, you may even notice that some newborns appear to have tiny raised breasts. This and any milk leakage is completely normal, and will not last beyond a few weeks. The reason behind this occurrence is that newborns absorb some of mom's estrogen hormones while they're in the womb. In baby daughters, it can also lead to vaginal discharge or mini periods.

10. **Most newborns like facing the right side when they sleep.** And many experts think this may be linked to why most people are right-handed. Only about 15% babies prefer to face the left side when they sleep.

11. **They can remember what you ate while you were pregnant with them.** And most fascinating of all, this may influence their own personal flavor preferences. Everything that mom eats after four months of pregnancy affects the way their amniotic fluid tastes and they'll know instantly when this same flavor comes up again in mom's breastmilk. If mom ate a lot of meals with heavy garlic flavoring, you can bet that baby will be drawn to garlic later on.

6 Must-Know Rules About Formula-Feeding

1. **Do not reuse formula your baby doesn't finish, even if you refrigerate it first.** It becomes a breeding ground for bacteria after a certain time and this is not helped by storing it. If, however, you've prepared formula that your baby never even touches the nipple of, then it's safe to store for 24 hours. Do

not do this if your baby has had his or her mouth on the bottle's nipple at all.

2. **Do not use prepared formula that's been left out for more than an hour.** The bacteria that grows beyond this time can make your baby ill.

3. **Store formula in the back of your fridge, which is where it is coldest** – but do *not* freeze formula. Freezing formula negatively affects its texture and consistency. While this isn't dangerous, you baby will be far less likely to drink it this way.

4. **Serve formula as soon as it's prepared and warmed.** As soon as it has time to sit, bacteria starts to accumulate. Give it to your baby before it has time to become a breeding ground.

5. **Be a total clean freak when it comes to your baby's formula.** This is one of the few times it's completely appropriate to go nuts over every detail. Make sure you wash your hands before handling your baby's formula and the counter on which it's being prepared. In addition to this, always clean and then properly dry the lid of your formula. Like I said, be a clean freak!

6. **Do not heat up formula in the microwave.** Doing this will heat the formula up unevenly, making extremely hot spots in the solution which are likely to burn your baby's mouth. The best way to heat up formula is with a bottle warmer. If you don't intend on purchasing one, leave bottled formula to stand in a bowl of hot water for just a few minutes. This should do the trick!

Foods to Limit or Avoid While Breastfeeding

You may not be pregnant anymore, but if you're breastfeeding, your baby will still affected by what you eat and drink. For this reason, you'll need to watch what enters your body. Not everything on this list needs to be completely eliminated from your diet; you'll just need to moderate the amount you eat or do so with precaution. Foods you need to limit will not harm your baby in any way, but they may bring about an undesired reaction or behavior, making it more difficult for mom and dad to establish a healthy dynamic. It is important to note that every baby is different and some 'foods to limit' may be more compatible with your newborn.

Foods to Limit or Moderate

- **Spicy Food**

Hot spices can have an affect on how your milk tastes and interacts with your baby's system. Most babies can handle it, but in large amounts or too much frequency, it may induce, colic, gas, or even diarrhea. Some babies are less tolerant towards spice so always pay close attention to see what your baby can handle.

- **Certain Herbs**

Herbs such as peppermint, sage, thyme, oregano, and parsley should be used sparingly. While they aren't dangerous to the baby in any way, they are well-known to reduce a mother's milk supply. On the other hand, feel free to enjoy them if you're struggling with an oversupply of milk or trying to wean your baby off breast milk.

- **'Gassy Vegetables'**

No mom should flat out avoid gassy vegetables, but in the early days, you may need to watch your baby to see how he or she reacts. Gassy vegetables include onions, broccoli, cabbage, cauliflower, peppers, and garlic; some babies can handle these just fine, but others can get extremely uncomfortable and gassy.

- **Caffeine**

Breastfeeding mothers still have to avoid caffeine, but they can consume about 100g more than they used to. This said, some moms choose to opt out of caffeine since it can give their baby sleep problems and make them very fussy. Remember that caffeine isn't just in coffee, it's also in chocolate, energy drinks, and certain teas.

- **Alcohol**

Doctors still say the safest option is to avoid alcohol, but breastfeeding mothers no longer *have* to. There are very reliable ways to get a drink in without it affecting the baby. Breastfeeding mothers should limit themselves to a small glass of wine or a half-pint of beer a day and absolutely no more than that. As with everything in your diet, alcohol can pass through your breast milk to your baby. It hasn't proven to be harmful in very small amounts, so it's essential that mothers limit how much gets through. They can do so by:

I. Waiting at least three hours after drinking to breastfeed the baby.

II. Drinking while breastfeeding, as it takes about 25 minutes for alcohol to enter breast milk.

III. Feeding the baby from stored breast milk when alcohol is still in mom's system.

It's also important that mothers stick to their alcohol limit per day. The more alcohol is consumed in one sitting, the longer it stays in your system.

Foods to Avoid

This one is simple: avoid all other foods that were in the 'Quit List' in Chapter 1. This means no high-mercury fish or unpasteurized dairy. If you're a seafood lover, make sure tuna, swordfish, mackerel, and shark are off your plate. And if you're a cheese nut, always check if it's pasteurized first.

How to Prevent Sudden Infant Death Syndrome

Sudden Infant Death Syndrome, also known as SIDS or Crib Death, is easily every parent's worst nightmare. It is the name given to the spontaneous death of a sleeping baby under one year-old. What makes SIDS even more harrowing is the fact that experts still aren't sure why it happens and there are no warning signs to watch out for. Unfortunately, there is no sure way to prevent SIDS, but you can take measures to lower your baby's risk. The good news is that these preventative measures seem to work; the SIDS rate has dropped by over 60% since they were made official to the public. Here are the best tips available on how to safeguard against SIDS:

1. **Lay your baby to sleep on a firm and bare mattress.** Even though it may seem as if an adorable little human needs something soft, firm mattresses are actually the best choice for SIDS prevention. Soft and fluffy paddings or quilts actually raise the chance suffocation or smothering. All you need is a firm mattress and a fitted sheet or a simple bassinet. And yes, this does mean *no* soft toys or crim bumpers.

2. **Put your baby to sleep on his or her back.** During the first year, they should never at any point be put to sleep on their side or stomach. If anyone else is taking care of your baby, it's important that you let them know this important detail as well. Many sitters believe that a fussy baby can be calmed if they're left on their stomach; whether or not this is true, the raised risk of SIDS means it is not worth finding out. Don't assume that every child care provider knows this and always let them know.

3. **Breastfeed your baby for as long as possible.** Even if you plan on formula-feeding eventually, see how long you can keep breastfeeding part of your baby's routine. Ideally, you should do this for six months, if you can. Remarkably, experts have found that breastfed babies have up to 50% of a lower risk of getting SIDS. The reasons why aren't very clear but it may be due to the fact that breast milk protects babies from infections, some of which could be responsible for SIDS. All this said, a breastfeeding mother that drinks alcohol actually raises her child's risk.

4. **Do not let your newborn sleep in the same bed as mom, dad, or another child.** While it's completely fine to cuddle and feed your baby in bed, avoid falling asleep together as this, too, raises the risk of suffocation and smothering. Accidents have occurred where a sleeping parent rolls against or onto their baby, restricting their breathing. Avoid this risk by sleeping in separate beds and not breastfeeding your baby in a position where you may fall asleep.

5. **Keep baby's crib in mom's bedroom.** Studies have shown that a baby who sleeps in mom's bedroom (but not in her bed) has a lower risk of SIDS. For this reason, experts tend to advise

that newborns don't sleep in their own room until they're older than six months.

6. **Absolutely do not smoke around your baby.** Secondhand smoke is another major risk factor for SIDS. If a smoker is going to be around your baby, make sure that they do not smoke anywhere near the baby. If it helps, let them know of the risks so that they understand what's at stake.

7. **Make sure your baby doesn't overheat.** As you'd expect, overheating increases a baby's risk of SIDS. When your baby goes to sleep, have him or her dressed in comfortable clothes made of a light material. And as long as the room temperature is comfortable for an adult, then it's perfect for your baby.

8. **Don't give honey to an infant.** In very young children, honey can lead to an illness called botulism. While more research needs to be done on this subject, there is evidence to suggest that botulism is linked to SIDS.

And a final note: there are many products out there that wild claims about being able to lower a baby's SIDS risk – keep in mind that these are *just* wild claims. There is no evidence that any of these products, including electronic respirators and cardiac monitors, are effective or even safe.

It's Bath Time!

Bath time can be an incredibly fun and adorable experience with a newborn; you'll be pleased to know that this ritual only gets cuter as they get older. But when things get wet and slippery, the chance of an accident happening gets even higher. This is why it's very important that parents are prepared and attentive during their child's bath time.

Follow these tips to make sure bath time is safe, efficient, and comfortable for your baby.

- **Establish a bathtime routine**

Choose a time of day that works for baby's bath time and try to stick to that routine. It's the best way to start setting your baby's body clock. Many moms prefer an evening bathtime routine since the time spent in water is very relaxing and sometimes makes baby sleepy. Over time, they begin to make the connection between bathtime and sleeptime, understanding that these activities go hand and hand. But this said, it's completely up to you and what works for your lifestyle. Morning bath routines are just as wonderful! And remember that just because you've established a routine doesn't mean you have to follow it religiously; if baby is hungry and bathtime needs to be postponed, that's fine too!

- **Have everything you need closeby**

Think of all the supplies you'll need while washing your baby and for right after, and have them within arm's reach. The last thing you want to do is to gather up your wet newborn mid-bath to rush to a different room. Make it easy on yourself! Have all bath time products and drying essentials ready nearby.

- **Water should be warm but not hot**

Before putting baby in the bath, test the water temperature with your elbow, one of the body's more sensitive areas. The water needs to be comfortably warm – not hot and not cold – around 98-100 °F. In order to get just the right temperature, I advise running the cold water first and the hot water after. Do not put your baby in running water. Being exposed to too-hot water for just a second can be enough to scald baby's skin. If you can, also try to keep the room temperature relatively warm, as naked babies can lose body heat very quickly.

- **Don't leave your baby sitting in water for too long**

Ideally, bath time should be at least five minutes and no longer than ten. When babies are left in water for too long, their skin becomes at risk of drying out, especially since it's already pretty dry. In extreme cases, babies can even catch hypothermia, a condition caused by losing body heat faster than you can produce it. And needless to say, you should also not leave your baby sitting or lying in water unattended. You must always stay present during your baby's bath.

- **Use a mild and baby-friendly soap**

A baby's skin is sensitive; for bath times, only use gentle soaps that are, ideally, free of fragrances. The chemicals and oils that are in mom and dad's soap are likely to irritate their skin – even if the packaging looks inviting! To safeguard against skin irritation, I'd even advise using just a small amount of soap and only using it towards the end of bath time. When a baby sits in soapy water for too long, irritation can also develop that way.

- **Wash baby girls from front to back**

This isn't just a tip for bath time, it is also an important piece of advice for diaper-changing. Whether you're wiping or washing a baby girl, you should always go from front to back. This is to avoid anything harmful from getting into her most sensitive area. To be extra safe, you should also steer clear of using soap on her vagina, as oftentimes this can lead to skin irritation.

- **Do not put newborns in a bath seat or ring**

In fact, all babies under one year-old should not be in a bath seat. The reason is simple: these babies are just too small for a bath seat. Too-little babies can easily slide out of the seat since they aren't yet able to fully support themselves. And on top of this, bath seats can easily collapse, potentially leading to the submersion of a baby's face in water. It's also possible for babies to get stuck in or under these unwieldy contraptions. At this point in your child's life, the support of mom or dad's arms are more than enough to keep them safe and comfortable. Sometimes 'simple' really is better.

By now, I don't need to tell you that raising a newborn is hard work. There's a lot of information out there about how to do it right – at the end of the day, what matters most of all is what's safest for your baby.

Enjoy these precious moments with your newborn baby. If there's anything that has struck me about having a newborn baby, it's this: time goes by so fast! In fact, the newborn stage doesn't seem to last long at all. Before you know it, you have a toddler and then a smart-mouthed kid (or at least I do!), and you're left wondering, "Where did all that time go?"

So, as stressed-out and exhausted as you are, take the time to snap a mental picture of these early days. You'll cherish these memories forever.

Conclusion

Congratulations on making it to the end of *First Time Mom*! One of the best things you can do as a new parent is to stay informed; that's what you've done by finishing this book! You are leaps and strides closer to being the best parent you can be for your little one. Many new moms feel overwhelmed by how much information there is to read and remember. Just know that your immediate concerns should be eating well, staying away from harmful activities, and taking care of yourself. To lighten the load off your shoulders, I even recommend passing this book on to your birth partner or closest family member. This way you can both be aware of the best way to take care of you and the baby.

I've walked you through the details of each and every trimester. By now, you'll know all about your expected symptoms and you'll have picked up some tricks about how to manage them. You'll know what supplements to include in your diet, how to control your pregnancy weight, and how to take care of your skin to minimize the chance of stretch marks. In the early days, your body will be going through some big adjustments; by now, you'll know what these changes are. If you feel like you need someone else on board for some extra support, go ahead and begin the search for a doula! Especially for a first-time mom, a doula can make a world of difference to your first pregnancy experience.

Remember to start your pelvic floor exercises in the second trimester – that is, if you've decided to do them. It's completely optional, but they'll be highly valuable in preventing incontinence. Preeclampsia symptoms can show up as early as the second trimester, so if you notice any unusual symptoms, refer back to the preeclampsia section to see how many signs you check off. You're probably okay, but reach out to a doctor immediately if you're unsure. It's always best to be safe!

When the third trimester rolls around, it's about time to start preparing for your big day and your new life with your baby. Decide whether you'd like to breastfeed or formula-feed your baby. Make sure you have everything or at least most of the things on the 'Necessities' list. You won't want to go out shopping when your newborn arrives, so it's best to get that out of the way now! You can also prepare for your big day by creating a birth plan, but this isn't necessary. It's just a way for you to establish what you want for your big day and to ensure those wishes are met.

If you have a doula, she'll be able to tell you when you're in labor and when you need to go to the hospital. If you don't, then make sure you pay close attention to what the most common labor signals are. You should also know how to tell the difference between Braxton Hicks contractions and real labor contractions. You don't want to end up going to the hospital for nothing!

Eventually, your big day will come and your little one will be ready to be born. Whether you plan on a vaginal birth or a C-section, childbirth is rarely easy. Stay fully informed about what you can expect. If you're having a vaginal birth, read up on epidurals so you know whether you'd like one. Keep in mind that you may change your mind at the last minute, if the pain is intense. There's nothing wrong with this!

You'll feel a rollercoaster of emotions in the days following your child's birth. There will be overwhelming joy, but many mothers also develop the baby blues and postpartum depression. Don't feel guilty or ashamed if you have your low moments. This is normal. Seek out help if you feel you may have postpartum depression. It's easily treated in this day and age. Take care of your emotional health and also take care of your physical well-being. Do not stress your body out or perform rigorous exercise for a while. Focus on eating well, sleeping, and nursing your baby. Get all the help you need from your friends and family. And remember that self-care is extremely important for the recovering first-time mom!

Of course, the journey doesn't end once you give birth. This may seem like a lot already, but all of this counts as step one. Motherhood begins here. When you have your newborn baby in your arms, it'll feel like a new day has started and in many ways, it has. No mother will ever be 100% prepared because every baby is different, so when all else fails, focus on the core things: baby's food, sleep, and safety – and yours as well. You're not alone in this! Refer back to this book whenever you need to and don't be afraid to ask your partner for help.

Welcome to the beautiful and empowering journey of motherhood, first-time mom! You've done an incredible job. I wish you and your new family happiness, health, and a lifetime of fun adventures together.

30 Day Meal Plan

Week 1

	Breakfast	Lunch	Dinner
Day 1	Oatmeal with blueberries, sliced apple, and a pinch of cinnamon.	A peanut butter and banana sandwich made with whole-wheat bread.	Salmon with a side of baked broccoli and potatoes.
Day 2	Greek yogurt and berries of choice.	A cooked-turkey wrap with swiss cheese, avocado, spinach, and hummus.	Cooked shrimp (deveined and peeled) with broccoli, cauliflower, garlic, and tomatoes in olive oil.
Day 3	A smoothie made of bananas, raspberries, chia seeds, and low-fat vanilla yogurt.	A baked potato with butter and cheddar cheese.	Pasta in a light olive oil or butter sauce with spinach, mushrooms, and pine nuts, topped with parmesan cheese.
Day 4	An omelette with cheddar cheese and toasted whole-wheat bread, lightly	An arugula and fig salad topped with balsamic vinegar, walnuts, and	Pork chops, green beans, and mashed sweet potatoes.

		buttered.	parmesan.	
Day 5		Granola with low-fat yogurt and berries of choice.	A spinach and cheese quiche with any salad of choice.	Chicken tenders in a lemon sauce, topped with parmesan, with a side of brussel sprouts.
Day 6		A peanut butter, banana, milk, and spinach smoothie.	Avocado toast with a sprinkle of salt and pepper.	Roasted chicken with baked baby potatoes, asparagus, and carrots.
Day 7		Broccoli and cheddar cheese omelette.	Creamy butternut squash soup.	Garlic, shrimp, and mushroom quinoa cooked in vegetable broth.

Week 2

	Breakfast	Lunch	Dinner
Day 8	Scrambled eggs on whole-wheat toast with baked beans on the side.	A chicken salad with sliced avocado, spinach, parmesan, olive oil, and balsamic vinegar.	Beef liver, onions, and mushrooms with a side of brown rice.

Day 9	Oatmeal with two sliced bananas.	An egg wrap with cheddar cheese, spinach, and salsa.	Chicken cutlets in a mushroom sauce with peas and carrots.
Day 10	A smoothie made of bananas, pears, chia seeds, and low-fat vanilla yogurt.	Broccoli and pea soup with optional whole-wheat toast for dipping.	Lamb chops with a side of asparagus and sweet potato wedges.
Day 11	Greek yogurt and berries of choice.	A baked potato with cottage cheese.	Broccoli, spinach, and sweetcorn pasta bake with cheese.
Day 12	Spinach and cottage cheese omelette.	A peanut butter and banana sandwich made with whole-wheat bread.	Chicken soup with carrots and celery.
Day 13	Low-fat yogurt with sliced mango and banana.	A cooked-turkey wrap with swiss cheese, avocado, spinach, and hummus.	Salmon with a side of kale cooked in lemon and garlic.
Day 14	Granola with low-fat yogurt and berries of choice.	Spinach and edamame salad with grated carrots, parmesan shavings,	Mushroom and chicken risotto made with brown rice.

| | | and sweet corn with a citrus dressing. | |

Week 3

	Breakfast	Lunch	Dinner
Day 15	A smoothie made of kale, avocado, bananas, pineapple, and chia seeds.	A baked sweet potato stuffed with spinach, avocado, and topped with a sunny side up egg.	Pesto pasta with garlic, peas, and sun-dried tomatoes.
Day 16	Whole-wheat waffles topped with honey and sliced banana.	A walnut, pear, and feta cheese (pasteurized) salad.	Spaghetti bolognese.
Day 17	Sunny side up eggs with a side of mushrooms, spinach, and tomatoes.	Lentil soup with carrots, garlic, potatoes, carrots, and parmesan shavings on top.	Garlic, shrimp, and mushroom quinoa cooked in vegetable broth.
Day 18	Broccoli and cheddar cheese omelette.	Creamy butternut squash soup.	Chicken thighs baked with artichoke, peas, garlic, and onions.

Day 19	Whole-wheat toast with banana and peanut butter or other nut butter.	Feta, spinach, and mushroom quiche.	Pork chops, green beans, and mashed sweet potatoes.
Day 20	A peanut butter, banana, milk, and spinach smoothie.	A chicken salad with sliced avocado, spinach, parmesan, olive oil, and balsamic vinegar.	Grilled salmon in a buttery lemon sauce with a side of chopped baby potatoes and asparagus.
Day 21	Avocado toast with a sprinkle of salt and pepper.	An egg wrap with cheddar cheese, spinach, and salsa.	A mushroom, spinach, celery, and cheese pasta bake.

Week 4

	Breakfast	Lunch	Dinner
Day 22	Spinach and cottage cheese omelette.	An arugula and fig salad topped with balsamic vinegar, walnuts, and parmesan.	Meatballs in tomato sauce with a side of mashed potatoes and broccoli.

Day 23	Oatmeal with blueberries, sliced apple, and a pinch of cinnamon.	Broccoli and pea soup with optional whole-wheat toast for dipping.	Chicken tenders in a lemon sauce, topped with parmesan, with a side of brussel sprouts.
Day 24	Sunny side up eggs with a side of mushrooms, spinach, and tomatoes.	A peanut butter and banana sandwich made with whole-wheat bread.	Cooked shrimp (deveined and peeled) with broccoli, cauliflower, garlic, and tomatoes in olive oil.
Day 25	Granola with low-fat yogurt and berries of choice.	A baked sweet potato stuffed with spinach, avocado, and topped with a sunny side up egg.	Beef liver, onions, and mushrooms with a side of brown rice.
Day 26	Egg, bean, and cheese breakfast burrito.	Spinach and edamame salad with grated carrots, parmesan shavings, and sweet corn with a citrus dressing.	Mushroom and chicken risotto made with brown rice.
Day 27	A smoothie made of kale, avocado, bananas, pineapple, and	Avocado toast with a sprinkle of salt and pepper.	Chicken cutlets in a mushroom sauce with peas and carrots.

	chia seeds.		
Day 28	Sliced peaches and mango in low-fat yogurt.	A pork and spinach salad with figs, red grapes, balsamic, honey, and pasteurized goat or feta cheese.	Pesto pasta with garlic, peas, and sun-dried tomatoes.

Week 5

	Breakfast	Lunch	Dinner
Day 29	Oatmeal with two sliced bananas.	Sandwich made of whole-wheat bread with artichoke, spinach, swiss cheese, sliced red peppers and sun-dried tomatoes.	Roasted chicken with baked baby potatoes, asparagus, and carrots.
Day 30	A peanut butter, banana, milk, and spinach smoothie.	Lentil soup with carrots, garlic, potatoes, carrots, and parmesan shavings on top.	Chicken thighs baked with artichoke, peas, garlic, and onions.

Snack List

Any Week

A bowl of mixed fruit	Chips and guacamole	Roasted tomatoes topped with parmesan	Banana bread
Cheese (pasteurized) and Crackers	Almonds	Kale chips	Dried fruit and nuts
One or two hard-boiled eggs	Cottage cheese	Cucumber and carrot sticks with peanut butter	Sweet potato chips
Edamame	Bananas	Low-fat yogurt and cereal fortified with iron or fiber	Hummus and pita bread
Homemade iced tea with lemon	Oatmeal and raisins	Orange slices	Black bean and cheese quesadilla

www.ingramcontent.com/pod-product-compliance
Lightning Source LLC
Chambersburg PA
CBHW022008120526
44592CB00034B/741